Summary

Temporal Mastery: Harnessing Every Second

Proven Techniques and Transformative Habits for Optimal Productivity and Balance

Alexander J. Graham

Chapter 1: Foundations of Temporal Mastery

In an ever-evolving world where time seems to be slipping through our fingers, the concept of temporal mastery has become more crucial than ever before. Our ability to effectively manage our time can greatly impact our productivity, success, and overall satisfaction in life. This first chapter of our book aims to delve into the foundational principles of temporal mastery, exploring the various aspects that contribute to this essential skill.

Understanding the Nature of Time:

Time is an enigmatic force, universally experienced yet often undervalued. To truly master time, we must first comprehend its nature. Time is not merely a measurement; it is a resource—an asset that we possess and must invest wisely. While time is constantly moving forward, we have the power to shape and navigate it in a way that aligns with our goals and aspirations, rather than being swept away by the rapid current.

Awareness: Keys to Unlocking Temporal Mastery:

At the core of achieving temporal mastery lies self-awareness. We must cultivate a deep understanding of our own temporal patterns, strengths, and weaknesses. By acknowledging our natural inclinations towards procrastination, distraction, or inefficient use of time, we can lay the foundation for improvement.

Self-awareness begins with recognizing our individual chronotypes, the biological predispositions that dictate our energy levels and focus throughout the day. Identifying whether we are early birds or night owls allows us to strategically plan our activities and allocate the most demanding or important tasks during peak performance hours.

Moreover, embracing mindfulness practices can significantly enhance our temporal awareness. By grounding ourselves in the present moment, we become acutely attuned to our use of time, making intentional choices rather than being swept away by unconscious habits. Mindfulness trains our minds to stay focused and avoid distractions, enabling us to make the most of each passing second.

Goal Setting: The North Star of Temporal Mastery:

An integral aspect of temporal mastery lies in setting clear, realistic, and well-defined goals. Goals act as our guiding lights, directing our actions and decisions, and helping us optimize our temporal resources. However, goal setting is not a one-time endeavor; it requires ongoing revision and adaptation as circumstances change.

To effectively set goals, we can utilize the SMART framework - Specific, Measurable, Achievable, Relevant, and Time-bound. Breaking down our larger aspirations into smaller, actionable steps allows for greater clarity in execution, preventing us from being overwhelmed by large tasks. Regularly reassessing and refining our goals ensures that we remain on track and in pursuit of meaningful outcomes.

Planning and Prioritization: The Architect of Time:

Skillful planning and prioritization are the architects of temporal mastery. Without a solid blueprint, time can often slip through our fingers, leaving us feeling aimless and unproductive. By developing effective planning strategies, we can align our actions with our goals, optimizing our use of time.

The Eisenhower Matrix, a tool made famous by former US President Dwight D. Eisenhower, is a useful technique for prioritizing tasks. The matrix categorizes tasks into four quadrants based on their urgency and importance. By focusing on tasks that are both urgent and important, we avoid falling into the trap of busyness-driven productivity and instead invest our time in activities with the highest impact.

Additionally, adopting effective time-blocking techniques can exponentially improve our ability to manage and compartmentalize our daily activities. By setting aside dedicated blocks of time for specific tasks or themes, we can minimize multitasking and foster deep focus, increasing our productivity and efficiency.

Managing Distractions: Taming the Time-Thieves:

In today's digital age, distractions abound, threatening our temporal mastery at every turn. To address this challenge, we must develop effective strategies to manage distractions and protect our precious time. One technique known as attention management involves consciously directing our focus towards the activities that truly matter.

Creating a distraction-free environment is essential for minimizing interruptions and promoting deep work. By reducing external noise and implementing digital detoxes, we can shield ourselves from the constant influx of notifications and temptations vying for our attention.

Moreover, technological tools can also aid in managing distractions. Various apps and browser plugins offer features that minimize or block time-wasting websites or social media platforms, allowing us to regain control over our online behavior. By using these tools selectively and intentionally, we create an environment conducive to temporal mastery.

The Philosophy Behind Time

Time is an elusive concept that has captivated humanity for centuries. From philosophers to physicists, thinkers have attempted to comprehend and explain the nature of time. In this chapter, we will explore the philosophy behind time, delving into its various interpretations and the profound implications it holds for our understanding of reality.

The Flowing River:

One of the ancient philosophical views of time is akin to a flowing river. This perception suggests that time moves continuously, flowing past us like water. This metaphorical image implies that the past is irretrievable while the future remains uncertain and untapped. This view, often associated with Heraclitus, emphasizes the impermanence of existence, with each moment fading away into the ever-advancing river of time.

Time as a Linear Sequence:

Another perspective on time proposes that it follows a linear sequence, in which events occur one after another, progressing indefinitely into the future. This notion of an arrow-like time exhibits a sense of directionality, suggesting an inherent order and progression from the past to the future. This view aligns with our everyday experience and has influenced countless philosophical and scientific inquiries into the nature of cause and effect.

The Eternal Present:

Contrasting the linear sequence, some philosophies posit that time is an illusion and that only the present moment exists. This view, closely related to the teachings of Eastern philosophies such as Buddhism and Taoism, argues that the past and future are mere constructions of the mind. By focusing on the present, proponents of this perspective advocate mindfulness and the attainment of a deeper understanding of ourselves and the world around us.

The Block Universe:

One of the more perplexing notions regarding time is the concept of the block universe. According to this view, time is not experienced as a flow or a sequence of moments but rather as a static four-dimensional block, encompassing all events past, present, and future. This idea, strongly associated with the theory of special relativity in physics, challenges our conventional understanding of time as a dynamic force, instead presenting time as a fixed structure that we traverse.

The Illusion of Time:

Building upon the idea of the block universe, some philosophers argue that time itself is an illusion, a construct of the human mind. This perspective finds resonance with certain interpretations of quantum mechanics, suggesting that time is a subjective experience rather than an objective reality. This concept links to the widely debated notion that our understanding of time is limited and that it may fundamentally differ from the true nature of the universe.

The Arrow of Time:

In addition to these diverse metaphysical views, the arrow of time is a phenomenon that has fascinated both philosophers and physicists alike. Time's arrow refers to the observed directionality of certain processes, such as aging or the apparent irreversibility of cause and effect. Despite the symmetrical nature of the fundamental laws of physics, the arrow of time implies an inherent directionality that distinguishes the past from the future and establishes a sense of order in our experience.

The Paradoxes of Time:

The study of time is not without its paradoxes, challenging our perceptions and deepening our philosophical ponderings. One such paradox is the famous "grandfather paradox," which arises when considering time travel. If one were to travel back in time and prevent their own birth, a perplexing contradiction arises: How could they have traveled back in time if they were never born? The paradox highlights the intricacies and potential inconsistencies that accompany the philosophical exploration of time.

Implications and Reflections:

The profound inquiries into the nature of time have far-reaching implications for our understanding of reality. From our personal experiences and the passing of our lives to the workings of the universe itself, time shapes our existence in intricate ways. It underscores the fleeting nature of our mortality and raises questions about whether it is possible to transcend its grasp.

In this chapter, we have embarked upon a philosophical journey through various interpretations of time. From the flowing river to the block universe, time's enigmatic nature has challenged our perceptions and provoked profound questions about the nature of existence. Although no definitive conclusion can be drawn, the exploration of time invites us to expand our intellectual horizons and seek a deeper understanding of the intricacies of our universe and our place within it.

The Science of Circadian Rhythms

In the intricate web of life processes, one of the most fundamental and intriguing phenomenon is the circadian rhythms. These rhythms are like internal clocks that regulate various physiological, behavioral, and biochemical processes in living organisms. They play a pivotal role in our daily routines, such as sleep-wake cycles, hormone secretion, body temperature, and even our mood patterns. In this chapter, we will delve into the captivating science behind these rhythms, exploring their origin, functions, and the underlying mechanisms that keep them ticking. So, fasten your seatbelts and join us on this exciting journey through the enigmatic world of circadian rhythms.

The Discovery of Circadian Rhythms:

The concept of circadian rhythms has fascinated scientists for centuries. However, it was not until recent times that researchers began to understand the intricacies and mechanisms behind this phenomenon. The term "circadian" originated from the Latin words "circa" (meaning around) and "diem" (meaning day), emphasizing the approximately 24-hour cycle these rhythms follow.

In the late 17th century, French astronomer Jean-Jacques d'Ortous de Mairan made a significant contribution to the study of circadian rhythms. He observed the leaves of the Mimosa pudica plant opening and closing with remarkable consistency, even when kept in constant darkness. This groundbreaking observation suggested the presence of some endogenous timing mechanism governing the plant's behavior. It marked the starting point for understanding the existence of biological clocks in living organisms.

Functions of Circadian Rhythms:

Circadian rhythms play a vital role in synchronizing an organism's internal processes with the external environment. They help to anticipate regular environmental changes, such as day and night cycles, and subsequently orchestrate various physiological responses accordingly. These rhythms offer numerous advantages, including improved performance, energy conservation, and adaptation to seasonal variations.

One of the most well-known circadian functions is the regulation of sleep and wakefulness. Our sleep-wake cycles, controlled by the suprachiasmatic nucleus (SCN) in the brain's hypothalamus, follow a roughly 24-hour pattern. The SCN receives input from photoreceptors in the retina, which detect light levels and help regulate the release of melatonin—a hormone that influences sleep. This intricate interaction between external light cues and internal clockwork helps us maintain a regular sleep routine.

Circadian rhythms also impact various physiological processes, including metabolism and hormone secretion. They influence the level of alertness throughout the day, body temperature fluctuations, and even our cognitive abilities. Moreover, they affect the functioning of vital organs like the heart, liver, and kidneys, by orchestrating their activity patterns to optimize efficiency.

The Molecular Oscillators:

To fully grasp the science behind circadian rhythms, we must dig deeper into the molecular mechanisms driving these rhythms. At the heart of this intricate dance are autonomous oscillators—genes, proteins, and cellular machinery that generate the rhythmical fluctuations.

The discovery of the first circadian clock gene, named "per" (period), in fruit flies (Drosophila melanogaster) marked a pivotal breakthrough in unraveling the molecular basis of circadian rhythms. Jeffrey C. Hall, Michael Rosbash, and Michael W. Young were awarded the Nobel Prize in Physiology or Medicine in 2017 for this groundbreaking research. The per gene encodes the PER protein, which accumulates in the cell during the night and degrades during the day, forming a rhythmic feedback loop.

Similar oscillatory feedback loops have been identified across various organisms, including mammals. In mammals, the core molecular oscillator consists of several genes and proteins collectively referred to as the "molecular clockwork." Core components include proteins such as CLOCK and BMAL1, which form a complex and bind to specific regions of DNA, activating the transcription of "clock-controlled genes" (CCGs). These CCGs are responsible for orchestrating various cellular processes during different phases of the circadian cycle.

The Importance of Consistency:

Maintaining a consistent circadian rhythm is of utmost importance for overall health and well-being. Disruptions in these rhythms, such as due to shift work, jet lag, or irregular sleep patterns, can have profound consequences on both physiological and psychological levels.

Studies have shown that those who regularly disrupt their circadian rhythms are at a higher risk of developing various health conditions, such as obesity, diabetes, cardiovascular diseases, and mood disorders. These disruptions can also impair cognitive abilities, memory formation, and even decrease lifespan.

Therefore, it is crucial to establish healthy habits to ensure a well-functioning circadian system. Practicing good sleep hygiene, avoiding excessive exposure to artificial light at night, and maintaining a consistent sleep schedule are all essential steps to keep our internal clocks ticking optimally.

As we come to the end of this enlightening chapter on the science of circadian rhythms, we have explored the discovery, functions, and underlying molecular mechanisms driving these enigmatic cycles. From leaves folding in on themselves to the complex oscillation of genes and proteins, circadian rhythms are a testament to the intricate synchronization of life processes.

The remarkable consistency of these rhythms keeps us in harmony with the world around us. Understanding the science behind circadian rhythms not only deepens our appreciation for the complexity of life but also sheds light on the importance of maintaining healthy habits to safeguard our own well-being.

.

Time Perception and Reality

Time, a seemingly simple concept that permeates every aspect of our lives, is one of the most intricate phenomena to understand. It exists as an abstract notion without any physical form or substance, yet it shapes our perception of reality and governs our daily activities. In this chapter, we delve into the fascinating realm of time perception and explore its complexities, examining the interplay between our subjective experience and the objective nature of time. We will explore various psychological and philosophical perspectives, delving into the mysteries that lie beneath our perception of time and its profound implications for our understanding of reality.

The Subjectivity of Time

Have you ever noticed how time seems to fly by when you're engaged in an enjoyable activity? Conversely, it seems to crawl when you're waiting impatiently for something. This subjectivity of time is a fundamental aspect of our experience, as each passing moment is filtered through the lens of our consciousness. The famous adage "time flies when you're having fun" captures the essence of this phenomenon. Our perception of time is influenced by the level of engagement, attention, and emotional significance associated with the events that unfold within it.

Psychologist William James proposed the concept of "specious present" to explain this subjective experience of time. He argued that our perception of the present consists of both the immediate past (retention) and the immediate future (protention), with the "specious present" stretching over a short duration of time. This implies that our experience of the present is not a mere snapshot, but a dynamic and continuous stream that encompasses past, present, and future elements. Thus, our subjective experience of time is inherently warped, influenced by a multitude of factors that shape our perception.

Temporal Illusions

The subjectivity of time perception becomes even more apparent when delving into temporal illusions - instances where our perception of time deviates from objective reality. One such illusion is the "stopped clock illusion." Have you ever looked at a clock to check the time, only to find that the second hand momentarily appears to freeze? This illusion occurs due to our neural processing speeds, where the momentary attention shift required to focus on the clock disrupts our perception of the second hand's movement, creating the illusion of a temporary pause.

Another intriguing temporal illusion is the "filling-in" mechanism. Our eyes have blind spots, yet we are usually unaware of them because our brain compensates by "filling in" the missing visual information. In a similar way, when there are gaps or missing elements in our memory of an event, our brain fills in the time gaps with plausible information. This phenomenon, known as "temporal interpolation," illustrates the malleability of our memories and how time perception can be distorted.

The Relationship Between Attention and Time Perception

Attention, a cognitive process that allows us to selectively focus on specific stimuli, plays a significant role in shaping our perception of time. When we are engrossed in an activity, our attention is fully absorbed, leading to a distortion of time perception. This concept, known as "time dilation," was introduced by psychologist Mihaly Csikszentmihalyi, who described this state as "flow" - a complete immersion in a task that suspends the awareness of time passing.

Conversely, when we are bored or engage in mundane activities, our attention becomes divided, leading to a heightened awareness of time passing. Psychologist Marc Wittmann proposed that our perception of time is influenced by the amount of attentional resources allocated to the task at hand. When our attention is narrowly focused, time seems to pass faster, while a divided or wandering attention results in time feeling prolonged.

Philosophical Perspectives on Time

While psychology helps us understand our subjective experience of time, philosophy delves into the deeper questions surrounding its nature and reality. Two dominant philosophical positions on time are eternalism and presentism. Eternalism posits that past, present, and future events all exist equally in reality. This view suggests that time is like a vast landscape, with every moment spread out in a timeless manner. Presentism, on the other hand, argues that only the present moment is real, and the past is gone while the future is yet to come into existence. Thus, time is seen as a succession of discrete moments, with only the present being genuinely real.

Another philosophical concept that challenges our conventional understanding of time is the notion of "timelessness." Some argue that timelessness exists in certain realms, such as in the realm of mathematical truths or in religious or mystical experiences. In these contexts, time loses its linear progression, and the distinction between past, present, and future becomes irrelevant.

The Physics of Time

To understand the objective nature of time, we must turn to the realm of physics, where the concept of time becomes intertwined with the fabric of the universe. According to the theory of relativity, formulated by Albert Einstein, time is not an absolute entity but rather a dimension intertwined with space, forming the fabric of spacetime. It is a unified entity that becomes distorted and curved by massive objects, causing time to pass at different rates depending on the strength of the gravitational field.

Quantum mechanics introduces yet another peculiar aspect of time. The famous "arrow of time" - the observed phenomenon of time moving inexorably forward - is not a fundamental property of physics at the microscopic scale. The laws of physics at this level are time-symmetric, meaning they are equally valid when time flows forward or backward. However, macroscopic systems, including our daily experience, exhibit irreversibility and an arrow of time. The reason behind this discrepancy remains one of the unresolved mysteries in physics.

Time, though intangible and elusive, profoundly shapes our perception of reality. It is a deeply subjective experience that remains enigmatic even in the face of scientific and philosophical exploration. Our perception of time is molded by a plethora of psychological, physiological, philosophical, and physical factors, each contributing to the complex tapestry that binds our consciousness to the temporal dimension.

Temporal Values and Life Priorities

In our ever-changing world, time is perhaps our most valuable resource. We live in an age where everything seems to move at breakneck speed, and it often feels like we are constantly chasing after time, trying to fit in all the tasks, responsibilities, and experiences that life demands of us. Yet, in our pursuit of productivity and accomplishment, we often forget to consider how our temporal values and life priorities shape our overall well-being and happiness.

Defining Temporal Values

Temporal values refer to the importance we assign to various aspects of time in our lives. These encompass how we perceive and utilize our time, as well as the significance we place on different time-related experiences. For instance, some individuals prioritize efficiency and productivity, valuing their time mainly based on how much they can accomplish within a given period. Others may emphasize spontaneity and cherishing the present moment, prioritizing experiences over strict adherence to schedules. Understanding our temporal values is crucial as they influence our life choices and impact our overall fulfillment.

The Inner Struggle: Short-term vs. Long-term Perspectives

One of the key dilemmas we face in relation to temporal values is the constant tug-of-war between short-term and long-term perspectives. When we prioritize short-term gains and immediate gratification, we may find ourselves neglecting important long-term objectives such as personal growth, career advancement, or cultivating meaningful relationships. Conversely, a myopic focus solely on long-term objectives can cause us to overlook the joys and opportunities that arise in the present moment. Striking a balance between these perspectives is a delicate challenge, requiring us to assess our values, aspirations, and the potential consequences of our choices.

Cultural Influences on Temporal Values

Temporal values are not solely determined by individual preferences; they are also influenced by prevailing cultural norms. Different cultures have distinct attitudes towards time, which can greatly impact individuals' priorities and perspectives. For instance, cultures that value efficiency and punctuality may prioritize productivity, while cultures that embrace leisure and relaxation may prioritize quality of life experiences. Recognizing the impact of cultural context on our temporal values allows us to understand and appreciate diverse perspectives and helps us navigate cross-cultural interactions more effectively.

The Psychological Dimension: Time Orientation

In addition to cultural factors, our individual time orientation significantly shapes our temporal values. Psychologists have identified two main time orientations: past-focused and future-focused. Past-focused individuals tend to reminisce, learn from history, and prioritize traditions and heritage. They may value stability and find solace in familiar routines. On the other hand, future-focused individuals are motivated by their aspirations and actively plan for what lies ahead. They may be more inclined to take risks and embrace change in pursuit of their goals. Understanding our dominant time orientation can help us align our temporal values with our individual needs and aspirations.

Time as a Finite Resource

A fundamental aspect of temporal values is recognizing time as a finite resource. Unlike other resources that can be replenished or acquired, time cannot be reclaimed once it has passed. This recognition creates a sense of urgency and highlights the importance of making conscious choices about how we spend our time. When we acknowledge time's finite nature, we are more likely to prioritize experiences and relationships that bring us joy and fulfillment.

Life Priorities: The Essence of Meaning and Fulfillment

Temporal values ultimately shape our life priorities, defining what we consider paramount in our quest for meaning and fulfillment.

Identifying and reflecting on our life priorities enables us to make intentional decisions that align with our values. While these priorities may differ vastly from person to person, they often revolve around common themes such as relationships, personal growth, health, career, community, and spirituality. By consciously aligning our actions with our life priorities, we open the door to a more purposeful and fulfilling existence.

Reevaluating Temporal Values: A Path to Transformation

As we journey through life, it is crucial to periodically reevaluate our temporal values and life priorities. We change, our circumstances evolve, and our aspirations may shift. What brought us joy and fulfillment in the past may no longer resonate with us in the present. Engaging in this critical self-reflection allows us to realign our actions with our evolving values, ultimately leading to personal growth and transformation.

Understanding our temporal values and life priorities is a vital step towards leading a more meaningful and fulfilled life. By recognizing the inherent trade-offs between short-term gains and long-term aspirations, appreciating cultural influences, considering our individual time orientations, and embracing time as a finite resource, we can make intentional choices that align with our values. Refining our temporal values and life priorities is an ongoing process, requiring us to periodically reassess our ever-changing selves. Through this introspection, we unlock the potential for personal growth, joy, and a more authentic existence.

Chapter 2: Time Wasters and Barriers to Mastery

In the pursuit of mastery, one must be acutely aware of the various obstacles and time wasters that can hinder progress. From external distractions to internal barriers, this chapter will delve into the common challenges faced by individuals seeking to master their craft. By understanding and identifying these hurdles, we can develop strategies to overcome them and pave the way towards true mastery.

Section 1: External Time Wasters

1.1 Technology and Social Media

The rise of technology and social media has significantly impacted our ability to concentrate and focus on tasks at hand. With the constant barrage of notifications, endless scrolling feeds, and addictive features, it's no wonder that valuable time is often wasted on these platforms. In order to combat this, it is crucial to establish strict boundaries and discipline oneself by allocating specific times for technology usage, implementing digital detoxes, and creating dedicated workspaces free from distractions.

1.2 Procrastination

Procrastination is the nemesis of mastery. We all have experienced moments where we have put off important tasks in favor of more enjoyable or easier activities. Overcoming procrastination requires understanding the underlying reasons behind this behavior, such as fear of failure or lack of motivation. By adopting effective time management techniques such as the Pomodoro Technique, setting clear goals, and breaking tasks into smaller, manageable chunks, we can minimize procrastination and maximize productivity.

1.3 Multitasking

Contrary to popular belief, multitasking does not lead to improved productivity. In fact, studies have shown that attempting to juggle multiple tasks simultaneously can significantly diminish concentration and overall performance. To avoid falling into this trap, it is vital to prioritize tasks, create a well-structured schedule, and allocate focused blocks of time to each task individually. By embracing single-tasking, we can ensure that our attention remains undivided, enabling us to achieve mastery in a more efficient manner.

Section 2: Internal Barriers

2.1 Self-doubt and Perfectionism

Self-doubt and perfectionism can cripple even the most talented individuals on their path to mastery. The relentless pursuit of perfection often leads to a fear of failure and a reluctance to take risks. Overcoming these internal barriers requires a shift in mindset. Embracing a growth mindset, focusing on progress rather than perfection, and viewing failures as opportunities for learning are essential steps towards mastery. Additionally, seeking support and guidance from mentors or peers can provide valuable insights and help combat self-doubt.

2.2 Lack of Discipline and Consistency

Consistency is the key to mastery. Without discipline and a steadfast commitment to regular practice, progress will be hindered. Establishing a routine that includes specific time dedicated to deliberate practice is crucial. By setting clear goals and holding oneself accountable, even on days when motivation wanes, one can develop the discipline necessary to overcome challenges and reach new levels of mastery.

2.3 Lack of Focus and Concentration

In today's world filled with constant distractions, maintaining focus and concentration can be a significant challenge. To cultivate these essential skills, eliminating external stimuli and creating an environment conducive to deep work is vital. Practices such as mindfulness and meditation can also be incredibly helpful in training the mind to remain present and focused. By honing these abilities, one can improve one's capacity for sustained concentration, thereby accelerating the journey towards mastery.

Section 3: Strategies for Overcoming Time Wasters and Barriers

3.1 Goal Setting and Prioritization

Establishing clear goals and priorities is essential for combating time wasters. By identifying what truly matters and aligning our efforts towards these objectives, we can minimize distractions and maximize productivity. Breaking down long-term goals into smaller, actionable steps also allows for a sense of accomplishment and progress, further bolstering motivation.

3.2 Creating an Optimal Work Environment

Designing an optimal work environment can significantly enhance focus and productivity. This involves minimizing distractions, organizing workspaces, and cultivating an environment that fosters inspiration and creativity. Factors such as lighting, ergonomic furniture, and a clean, clutter-free workspace can make a substantial difference in promoting efficient work habits.

3.3 Time Management Techniques

Adopting effective time management techniques is crucial for overcoming time wasters. Techniques such as time blocking, the Eisenhower Matrix, and utilizing productivity apps or tools can help increase efficiency, minimize distractions, and ensure that valuable time is utilized effectively.

In the pursuit of mastery, it is imperative to recognize and address the time wasters and barriers that hinder progress. By acknowledging the external distractions and internal obstacles, individuals can develop strategies to overcome them. With discipline, focus, and a growth mindset, one can navigate these challenges and embark on a path towards true mastery. With each hurdle overcome, a step closer to achieving excellence is taken, opening up a world of endless possibilities.

Digital Distractions in the Temporal Realm

In today's fast-paced digital world, we find ourselves constantly bombarded with information and opportunities for distraction. Our smartphones, tablets, and laptops have become an extension of ourselves, offering a never-ending stream of notifications, updates, and entertainment options. As we navigate through this temporal realm of digital distractions, it has become imperative to understand the impact these distractions have on our lives and the ways we can effectively manage them.

1. The Rise of Digital Distractions

The advent of the internet and the subsequent rise of smartphones and social media platforms has revolutionized the way we interact with the world. With just a few taps on a screen, we can consume a limitless amount of content, connect with people from any corner of the globe, and engage in various forms of entertainment. However, this newfound connectivity has also exposed us to a myriad of digital distractions that can lure us away from our intended tasks.

2. The Science of Digital Distractions

Human beings have limited attention spans, and technology has exploited this vulnerability to keep us continuously engaged. The allure of these distractions lies in their ability to trigger a release of dopamine, a neurotransmitter associated with pleasure and reward. Every like, comment, or notification triggers a small surge of dopamine in our brains, making it difficult to resist the urge to check our devices repeatedly.

Furthermore, studies have shown that our brain's ability to multitask is greatly limited, and attempting to juggle multiple digital distractions simultaneously can significantly impair our cognitive abilities. This not only affects our productivity but also has long-lasting consequences on our overall mental well-being.

3. The Impact on Productivity

One of the most apparent consequences of digital distractions is a decline in productivity levels. Constantly switching between tasks due to distractions leads to reduced focus and increased mental fatigue. Being unable to concentrate fully on a single task hinders our ability to complete it efficiently and effectively.

Moreover, the constant presence of digital distractions has seeped into our professional lives, affecting our ability to meet deadlines, collaborate effectively, and maintain focused attention during important meetings or discussions. The long-term impact of diminishing productivity can have profound implications for individuals and organizations alike.

4. The Social Side Effects

While connectivity to the digital realm has allowed us to transcend geographical barriers and connect with a larger global community, it has also led to adverse social effects. The constant presence of digital distractions can hinder real-world communication, leading to a decline in deep, meaningful connections.

Furthermore, the rise of social media has created a culture of comparison and envy, where individuals constantly seek validation and recognition through the number of likes or followers they accumulate. This obsession with the digital persona not only fuels anxiety and depression but also isolates individuals from the present moment, hindering the development of genuine relationships.

5. Strategies for Managing Digital Distractions

To mitigate the negative impact of digital distractions, it is essential to develop strategies for managing them effectively. Here are a few practical tips that can help you master the art of digital self-control:

a) Practice Digital Detox: Set aside specific times during the day to disconnect from all digital devices. Engage in offline activities such as reading a book, going for a walk, or spending quality time with loved ones. Encouraging moments of mindfulness can help break the cycle of constant distraction.

b) Establish Boundaries: Limit the notifications you receive on your devices to only those that are truly important. Disable or minimize alerts from social media platforms or other non-essential applications. Take control of your technology rather than letting it control you.

c) Prioritize Tasks: Start your day by identifying the most important tasks that need to be completed. Avoid opening unnecessary applications or tabs that may tempt you to procrastinate. Focusing on one task at a time and utilizing time management techniques can greatly enhance productivity.

d) Create Digital-free Zones: Designate certain areas in your home or workspace as digital-free zones. This allows for dedicated time and space away from distractions, promoting better focus and concentration.

e) Practice Mindfulness: Cultivate mindfulness by being fully present in the moment. Pay attention to your surroundings, emotions, and thoughts without constant reliance on digital devices. Engaging in activities such as meditation or deep breathing exercises can help train your mind to be more focused and less susceptible to distractions.

Navigating through the temporal realm of digital distractions presents constant challenges in this ever-connected age. The impact on our productivity, mental health, and social interactions cannot be understated. However, by understanding the science behind digital distractions and implementing practical strategies, we can strive for a more balanced and mindful approach to technology. By consciously managing our digital interactions, we can regain control of our attention and reclaim the richness of the present moment. The journey towards digital self-mastery begins with recognizing the power of digital distractions and working towards reclaiming our focus and well-being in this rapidly evolving digital landscape.

Mental Blockages and Time Mismanagement

"Time management is an oxymoron. Time is beyond our control, and the clock keeps ticking regardless of how we lead our lives. Priority management is the answer to maximizing the time we have." - John C. Maxwell

Time, the great equalizer, is a finite resource available to all individuals. Each person has 24 hours in a day, 1,440 minutes, and 86,400 seconds to utilize. Yet, it often seems that some individuals effortlessly achieve their goals and make the most of their time while others struggle to even complete their to-do lists. Mental blockages and time mismanagement play a significant role in hindering our productivity and progress. In this chapter, we will explore the impact of mental blockages on our time management, why they occur, and importantly, strategies to overcome them.

Understanding Mental Blockages:

Mental blockages can be described as the invisible barriers that inhibit our ability to focus, think clearly, and make effective decisions. They are obstacles that prevent us from reaching our full potential, both personally and professionally. Blockages can manifest in various forms, such as fear of failure, perfectionism, lack of motivation, or feeling overwhelmed.

Fear of failure is a common mental blockage that holds many individuals back from taking risks and trying new things. This fear stems from the belief that failure equates to personal inadequacy or embarrassment. As a result, individuals may shy away from opportunities that could lead to growth and success.

Perfectionism, another common blockage, can paralyze individuals and detrimentally impact productivity. The pursuit of flawlessness often sets unattainable standards, leading to procrastination and indecisiveness. Instead of completing tasks, individuals may continuously fine-tune and revise, never feeling content with their work.

Lack of motivation can also act as a significant mental blockage. When individuals lack the drive to pursue their goals and complete necessary tasks, time begins to slip away. Procrastination sets in, and critical deadlines become a source of stress and anxiety.

Feeling overwhelmed is yet another mental blockage that leaves individuals feeling scattered, unable to prioritize and manage their time effectively. This arises when the sheer volume of tasks and responsibilities becomes insurmountable, causing individuals to feel paralyzed and unsure where to start.

Root Causes of Mental Blockages:

Understanding the root causes of mental blockages is vital in developing strategies to overcome them. While each individual may have unique triggers, certain common factors contribute to these blockages.

Past experiences and conditioning play a significant role in shaping our attitudes and beliefs. Unresolved past failures or traumatic events can create a fear of failure, hindering individuals from taking risks and embracing new challenges. Likewise, growing up in an environment that overly emphasizes perfectionism can lead to self-imposed high standards that are difficult to meet.

Lack of self-confidence is another contributing factor to mental blockages. When individuals doubt their abilities and self-worth, fear of failure becomes more prominent. The belief that achievements are beyond one's capabilities perpetuates a cycle of inaction and stagnation.

External factors, such as societal pressure and comparison, can also contribute to mental blockages. Constantly comparing oneself to others' achievements or feeling pressured to meet societal expectations can lead individuals to doubt their abilities and undermine their confidence.

Strategies to Overcome Mental Blockages:

While everyone experiences mental blockages to some extent, there are various strategies to overcome them and manage our time more effectively.

1. Identify and acknowledge blockages: Awareness is the first step towards change. Identify the specific mental blockages that hinder your productivity and reflect on their root causes. Acknowledge that these blockages exist and recognize their impact on your time management.

2. Set realistic goals: Establish clear and attainable goals to reignite motivation and guide your actions. Break larger tasks into smaller, manageable steps to prevent feeling overwhelmed. As you achieve these smaller milestones, your motivation will gradually increase.

3. Challenge the fear of failure: Embrace failures as stepping stones to success. Understand that failure is a natural part of growth and learning. By reframing failure as an opportunity to learn from our mistakes, we loosen the grip of fear and open ourselves up to new possibilities.

4. Cultivate self-compassion: Treat yourself with kindness and understanding. Accept that perfection is unattainable and that mistakes are an integral part of the learning process. Practice self-

compassion by acknowledging your efforts and celebrating small victories along the way.

5. Prioritize and delegate: Learn to prioritize tasks based on their importance and urgency. Delegate non-essential tasks to others when possible, allowing you to focus on activities that align with your goals and require your expertise.

6. Practice effective time management techniques: Utilize time management techniques such as the Pomodoro Technique, time-blocking, or the Eisenhower Matrix. These techniques help break tasks into manageable chunks, allocate time efficiently, and promote focus and productivity.

Achieving effective time management requires addressing mental blockages that hinder our productivity. By identifying and understanding these blockages, we become better equipped to overcome them and make the most of our precious time. Remember, time is a finite resource that we can never reclaim once lost. Embrace the strategies outlined in this chapter to overcome mental blockages, prioritize effectively, and ultimately manage your time in a way that maximizes your potential.

The Myth of Multi-tasking

In our fast-paced, modern society, the ability to handle multiple tasks simultaneously has become a badge of honor. We hail those who can effortlessly switch between projects, answer emails while on a conference call, and juggle various responsibilities with apparent ease. We admire those who can seemingly defy the limitations of human attention and concentration. But is this vaunted skill of multi-tasking truly as valuable as it seems?

The prevailing notion that multi-tasking is an effective and efficient way to get things done is a myth that needs to be debunked. Contrary to popular belief, our brains are not wired to handle multiple tasks simultaneously. Rather, engaging in multi-tasking leads to reduced productivity, increased errors, and heightened stress levels.

To understand the fallacy of multi-tasking, we must delve into the intricacies of the human brain. Our brains have evolved to focus on one specific task at a time, dedicating its resources fully to that task in order to achieve optimal performance. This is known as single-tasking, a concept deeply ingrained in our neurobiology.

When we attempt to multi-task, what actually occurs is not the execution of several tasks simultaneously, but rather, the rapid switching of attention between tasks. Each time we switch our focus, our brains need to disengage from the previous task, reorient, and refocus on the new one. This process, known as task-switching, generates a cognitive cost that hampers our efficiency and diminishes the quality of our work.

Studies have consistently shown that this constant toggling between tasks results in a significant decrease in productivity. Research conducted by neuroscientists at Stanford University revealed that individuals who engage in heavy multi-tasking actually perform worse on cognitive tasks compared to those who single-task. Despite the illusion of accomplishing more, multi-taskers tend to make more errors, experience memory lapses, and struggle with information recall.

Moreover, multi-tasking impacts our ability to engage in deep work—a state of focused and undistracted concentration necessary for producing high-quality work. Nobel Prize-winning economist Herbert A. Simon famously stated, "A wealth of information creates a poverty of attention." In an era where information overload is the norm, our attention becomes a precious commodity. Constantly diverting our attention between tasks, notifications, and distractions dilutes our ability to concentrate fully on the task at hand, preventing us from reaching our full potential.

The harmful effects of multi-tasking are not limited to diminishing productivity alone. Engaging in this practice has a profound impact on our psychological well-being. The more tasks we add to our plate, the more our stress levels escalate. Our brains are not designed to handle a constant stream of interruptions and shifting demands. The mounting pressure to stay on top of numerous tasks can lead to anxiety, burnout, and a decline in mental health.

One might argue that certain activities can be combined without hindering our performance, such as listening to music while doing chores or exercising while watching a documentary. While it is true that some simple and automatic tasks can be performed in conjunction with others, we need to be cautious when it comes to complex, cognitively demanding tasks.

Take, for instance, the case of driving while talking on the phone. Many people believe they possess the superhuman ability to drive safely while engaged in phone conversations. However, numerous studies have demonstrated that talking on the phone while driving impairs our attention to the road, resulting in delayed reaction times comparable to those exhibited by drunk drivers. The inescapable truth is that our brains cannot effectively allocate attention to both tasks at once, endangering ourselves and others in the process.

To break free from the allure of multi-tasking, we must cultivate the habit of deliberate single-tasking. By immersing ourselves fully in one activity, we can reap the benefits of enhanced focus, improved quality of work, and reduced stress levels. Here are a few strategies to help us transition from multi-tasking to single-tasking:

1. Prioritize tasks: Begin each day by identifying the most critical tasks that require your undivided attention. Focus on completing one task before moving on to the next. By intentionally selecting and sequencing tasks, you can ensure a smooth workflow and remain in control of your attention.

2. Create dedicated spaces: Set up physical or virtual spaces where you can work on specific tasks without distractions. Silence notifications, close unnecessary tabs on your computer, and communicate your need for uninterrupted time to your colleagues.

3. Practice mindfulness: Engaging in mindfulness exercises, such as deep breathing or meditation, can train your mind to be present and fully focused on the task at hand. Regular mindfulness practices can enhance your ability to concentrate and resist temptation.

4. Schedule breaks: Allowing yourself regular breaks throughout the day is essential. Fatigue and burnout can hinder productivity more than any other factor. Use these breaks to recharge, relax, and reset your mind before diving back into your work.

5. Cultivate patience: In a world that glorifies constant activity, it is crucial to recognize that focusing on a single task may require

patience. Many tasks demand time and effort to complete, and rushing through them will only compromise the quality of your work. Embrace the process, knowing that true productivity lies in doing one thing well, rather than many things poorly.

By embracing deliberate single-tasking, we can dismantle the myth of multi-tasking and reclaim control over our attention and productivity. Let us prioritize quality over quantity, depth over superficiality, and ultimately, well-being over the allure of false efficiency.

Reactive vs. Proactive Time Utilization

In our fast-paced world, time is an invaluable resource. How we choose to utilize our time can greatly impact our productivity, effectiveness, and overall well-being. One of the key factors in time management is understanding the difference between reactive and proactive time utilization. In this chapter, we will delve into the intricacies of these two approaches, their implications, and how they can shape our success in various areas of life.

Understanding Reactive Time Utilization:

Reactive time utilization refers to the tendency to respond to situations as they arise, often in a hurried and unplanned manner. This mode of operation is prevalent among individuals who prioritize short-term tasks and find themselves constantly putting out fires. Reactive time utilization is characterized by being highly responsive to external demands, interruptions, and distractions.

In the business world, a reactive approach often leads to a constant state of crisis management. When we spend most of our time reacting to unexpected issues, we are left with little time for long-term planning and strategic thinking. This can hinder our ability to innovate, make informed decisions, and achieve our goals effectively.

The Pervasive Nature of Reactivity:

The reactive mentality is not limited to the workplace; it can seep into other aspects of our lives as well. In relationships, many individuals adopt a reactive approach, merely responding to the needs and expectations of others without proactively communicating their own desires and needs. This can lead to a lack of fulfillment and resentment over time, as personal ambitions and aspirations fall by the wayside.

Reacting to external circumstances rather than taking charge can also impact our personal well-being. Whether it be failing to prioritize self-care, neglecting our physical health, or succumbing to the whims of others, a reactive mindset can severely limit our personal growth and hinder our overall happiness.

Challenges and Limitations of Reactive Time Utilization:

Reactive time utilization often leads to a host of challenges and limitations. Firstly, it fuels a perpetual state of busyness, leaving individuals feeling overwhelmed and burnt out. When we are constantly reacting to incoming tasks and distractions, there is little time for reflection, planning, and self-improvement.

Additionally, a reactive approach can hinder our ability to take advantage of opportunities. Opportunities often arise unexpectedly and require quick action. However, individuals accustomed to reacting may miss out on these chances due to a lack of preparedness or the inability to prioritize amidst the chaos of reactive time utilization.

Moreover, reactive time utilization tends to foster a sense of powerlessness. Those who rely on external demands to dictate their actions often lack a sense of control over their own lives, feeling tossed around by circumstance rather than steering their own ship. This can lead to increased stress, diminished self-confidence, and an overall negative impact on mental health.

Embracing Proactive Time Utilization:

In contrast to a reactive approach, proactive time utilization involves taking charge of our time and planning our actions in advance. Rather than being at the mercy of external demands, individuals who adopt a proactive mindset prioritize their long-term goals and take strategic steps to achieve them.

Planning and Goal Setting:

Fundamental to proactive time utilization is the art of planning and goal setting. By setting clear objectives, breaking down our goals into actionable steps, and scheduling them into our routine, we can ensure that we are dedicating time and attention to what truly matters. This proactive approach allows for focused efforts, increased productivity, and a sense of purpose.

Strategic Prioritization:

Proactive individuals understand the importance of prioritizing tasks based on their impact and alignment with long-term goals. They differentiate between urgent and important tasks and allocate time and energy accordingly. By prioritizing tasks proactively, individuals can prevent the sense of urgency that often accompanies reactive time utilization and perform at a higher level of efficiency.

Time Blocking:

An effective tactic employed by proactive individuals is time blocking. This technique involves assigning specific blocks of time to different tasks or areas of life, ensuring that we allocate adequate time to all essential aspects of our lives. Time blocking allows for increased focus, prevents multitasking, and ensures that we do not neglect important areas such as self-care, family, or personal development.

Proactive Communication:

One area where proactive time utilization makes a profound difference is in relationships, both personal and professional.

Proactive individuals not only communicate their own needs and expectations but also take the time to actively listen to others. By fostering open and proactive communication, they can build stronger connections, avoid misunderstandings, and work collaboratively towards shared goals.

Benefits of Proactive Time Utilization:

Adopting a proactive mindset offers numerous benefits across various areas of life. Firstly, proactive individuals experience a sense of control over their time and actions, creating a feeling of empowerment and confidence. By actively working towards their goals, they can make progress and feel a sense of accomplishment, which enhances motivation and fulfillment.

Proactive time utilization also allows individuals to capitalize and leverage opportunities. By having plans in place and remaining open-minded, proactive individuals can recognize opportunities as they arise and act decisively, making the most of favorable situations.

Furthermore, a proactive approach enables individuals to become more resilient to unexpected challenges. By planning for contingencies and anticipating potential difficulties, proactive individuals are better equipped to navigate obstacles, adapt to change, and maintain focus on their long-term objectives.

Chapter 3: Tools and Techniques for Time Optimization

In today's fast-paced world, time is a valuable resource. With so many tasks to accomplish and goals to achieve, finding ways to optimize our time becomes crucial. In this chapter, we will explore various tools and techniques that can help us effectively manage and make the most of our time. By implementing these strategies, we can increase our productivity, reduce stress, and achieve greater success in both our personal and professional lives.

Section 1: Time Management Tools

1.1 Digital Calendars and Time-Tracking Apps:

In an age where technology is at our fingertips, utilizing digital calendars and time-tracking apps can significantly improve our time management skills. These tools allow us to schedule and prioritize our tasks efficiently, set reminders, and track how we spend our time. Whether it's Google Calendar, Outlook, or Toggl, the key is to find the tool that best fits our needs and integrate it into our daily routine.

1.2 Task Management Tools:

Managing tasks effectively is essential for time optimization. Task management tools such as Trello, Asana, or Todoist provide a systematic approach to organizing and tracking our to-do lists. These tools allow us to break down our tasks into smaller, manageable steps, set deadlines, and collaborate with others. By using such tools, we can stay organized, focused, and ensure that nothing slips through the cracks.

1.3 Note-Taking and Documentation:

In any endeavor, taking notes and keeping track of important information is crucial. Tools like Evernote, OneNote, or Notion help us capture thoughts, ideas, and important details that can be easily accessed and retrieved when needed. These note-taking apps allow us to create searchable, organized digital notebooks, making it effortless to find and reference our notes, saving us valuable time and effort.

Section 2: Techniques for Time Optimization

2.1 Prioritization and Time Blocking:

One of the fundamental principles of time optimization is prioritization. By identifying our most important tasks and allocating time to focus on them, we can ensure that we spend our time wisely. Time blocking is a technique where we schedule specific blocks of time for various activities and prioritize tasks accordingly. By blocking distractions and dedicating uninterrupted time to essential tasks, we can achieve higher efficiency and productivity.

2.2 The Pomodoro Technique:

Developed by Francesco Cirillo in the late 1980s, the Pomodoro Technique is a time management method that splits work into intervals, typically 25 minutes long, separated by short breaks. By breaking our work into smaller, focused segments, we can enhance our concentration and eliminate burnout. The Pomodoro Technique is especially effective for tasks that require sustained attention and can be easily implemented using various timer apps or websites.

2.3 Time Tracking and Analysis:

To optimize our time, it is crucial to understand how we currently spend it. Time tracking involves recording the time spent on various activities, allowing us to identify time-wasting habits or inefficiencies. Tools like RescueTime, Toggl Track, or Clockify help us analyze our time usage patterns and identify opportunities for improvement. By gaining insights into our time allocation, we can make informed decisions and adjust our habits for better time optimization.

2.4 Delegation and Outsourcing:

Recognizing that we cannot do everything ourselves is an essential aspect of effective time optimization. Delegating tasks to others or outsourcing certain responsibilities allows us to focus on high-priority activities that require our expertise and attention. By leveraging the skills and capabilities of others, we not only lighten our workload but also create the opportunity for increased productivity and time efficiency.

2.5 Mindfulness and Mindset Shift:
While tools and techniques are valuable, it is equally important to cultivate a mindset that values time optimization. Practicing mindfulness, being fully present in the moment, can help us stay focused on the task at hand and avoid distractions. Additionally, adopting a growth mindset, embracing challenges, and viewing setbacks as learning opportunities can boost productivity and overall time management skills.

In this chapter, we delved into various tools and techniques that can aid in our journey towards time optimization. From digital calendars and task management tools to time-blocking and the Pomodoro Technique, these strategies empower us to take control of our time and make the most out of each day. By leveraging these tools and adopting effective techniques, we can enhance our productivity, reduce stress, and ultimately achieve greater success in both our personal and professional lives.

Time-Blocking Mastery

Time is a precious resource that slips through our fingers far too quickly. Each day, we find ourselves struggling to manage our ever-growing to-do lists and commitments, wondering where all the hours have gone. If only there were a way to extend the moments, to make every minute count – well, you're in luck! In this chapter, we will delve into the concept of time-blocking mastery, a powerful technique that will revolutionize the way you manage your time. Whether you're a busy professional, a student, an artist, or just someone seeking to regain control over your schedule, mastering the art of time-blocking will bring you closer to achieving your goals and living a fulfilling life. So, let's dive in!

Understanding Time-Blocking

Time-blocking is a time management technique that involves allocating specific periods, or blocks, of time to different activities or tasks. By adopting this practice, you can bid farewell to aimlessly drifting through your day, impeded by distractions and inefficiency. Time-blocking allows you to take charge of your schedule, enabling you to prioritize your most important tasks and ensure you have dedicated intervals for focused work.

Benefits of Time-Blocking

1. Enhanced Productivity: When you meticulously plan and allocate time for each task, you eliminate the ambiguity that often leads to procrastination. With time-blocking, you'll find yourself more motivated to get things done, leading to increased productivity.

2. Improved Focus: By dedicating specific slots of uninterrupted time to individual tasks, you'll experience a boost in concentration and focus. When distractions are minimized, you can immerse yourself fully in your work and achieve a state of flow.

3. Efficient Planning: Time-blocking allows you to develop a clear roadmap for your day, making it easier to set realistic goals and deadlines. With a well-structured schedule, you can ensure that every minute is allocated sensibly, avoiding the stress and overwhelm that often arises from poor time management.

4. Work-Life Balance: With time-blocking, you can strike a harmonious balance between work and personal life. By dedicating specific blocks for both professional and leisure activities, you'll be able to give your undivided attention to each aspect of your life, reducing stress and enhancing overall satisfaction.

5. Prioritization and Accountability: Time-blocking forces you to identify your most important tasks and allocate dedicated time slots

for them. This allows you to differentiate between urgent and non-urgent activities, ensuring that you focus on what truly matters. Moreover, once you've allocated specific blocks of time, you become accountable to yourself, increasing your commitment to complete the tasks at hand.

Implementing Time-Blocking Mastery

1. Set Clear Goals: Before you start time-blocking, it's crucial to establish clear, specific goals. What do you want to achieve in the next week, month, or year? Once you have a clear vision of your objectives, you can break them down into smaller, manageable tasks that can be time-blocked individually.

2. Create a Schedule: Designing an effective schedule is a key step in time-blocking mastery. Assess your energy levels and identify the times of day when you are most focused and productive. Allocate these prime hours to your highest-priority work. Additionally, ensure that you also allocate time for breaks, meals, exercise, and personal activities. Remember, a well-rounded schedule is vital for sustainable productivity.

3. Establish Time Blocks: Start by defining the duration of your time blocks. Common time blocks range from 30 minutes to two hours, depending on the nature and complexity of the task. Allocate blocks for frequently occurring activities that are necessary but not

demanding, such as checking emails or returning phone calls. Be flexible and adapt your time blocks as needed, but avoid excessive tweaking, as this can disrupt the flow of your day.

4. Avoid Overcommitment: While time-blocking allows you to maximize productivity, it's important not to overload your schedule. Be realistic about how much you can accomplish in a given block and allow for margin to handle unexpected tasks or delays. Overcommitting can lead to frustration, stress, and ultimately, abandoning the time-blocking practice altogether.

5. Minimize Distractions: During the allocated time blocks, be ruthless in minimizing distractions. Put your phone on silent or airplane mode, close irrelevant browser tabs, and create an environment conducive to focus. If necessary, communicate to those around you that you are not to be interrupted during these periods of dedicated work.

Time-blocking is a skill that requires practice, consistency, and flexibility. By mastering this technique, you can transform your relationship with time and reclaim control over your schedule. Implementing time-blocking mastery will enable you to prioritize tasks effectively, enhance productivity, and experience a sense of accomplishment. Remember, the key to success lies not in finding more hours in the day but in making the most of the ones we have. So why wait? Embrace time-blocking mastery and unlock the true power of your days!

The Pomodoro Technique and Time Intervals

In today's fast-paced world, where time is always at a premium, finding effective strategies to manage our time has become more important than ever. One such technique that has gained popularity over the years is the Pomodoro Technique. Developed by Francesco Cirillo in the late 1980s, this time management method has helped countless individuals enhance their productivity and focus. Central to its success is the concept of time intervals, which forms the foundation of the technique.

Chapter 1: Understanding the Pomodoro Technique

1.1 Origins and Background

The Pomodoro Technique takes its name from the Italian word for "tomato," inspired by the tomato-shaped kitchen timer that Cirillo used in his university days. What began as a personal method for Cirillo to keep track of his study sessions soon evolved into a fully-fledged technique. Its basic premise centers around breaking work into intervals, typically 25 minutes long, with short breaks interspersed between them.

1.2 The Technique in Practice

To implement the Pomodoro Technique, one must follow a simple set of steps. Firstly, identify the task to be accomplished. Next, set the timer for 25 minutes, known as a Pomodoro, and work solely on the chosen task until the timer rings. Once the Pomodoro is completed, take a short break of around five minutes before starting the next interval. After completing four Pomodoros, take a more extended break of about 15-30 minutes.

Chapter 2: The Power of Time Intervals

2.1 Harnessing Focus

One of the remarkable benefits of the Pomodoro Technique lies in its ability to enhance focus and concentration. By breaking work into manageable intervals, the technique prevents mental fatigue and burnout, keeping the mind fresh and agile. Working for short bursts also reduces the temptation to engage in distractions, ensuring that individuals remain undistracted and fully immersed in the task at hand.

2.2 Overcoming Procrastination

Procrastination is the nemesis of productivity, and many individuals struggle to overcome its clutches. Time intervals are an invaluable tool in combatting procrastination, as the time limits they impose instill a sense of urgency. Knowing that the clock is ticking motivates individuals to make the most of each Pomodoro and utilize their time efficiently.

2.3 Encouraging Efficiency

The Pomodoro Technique encourages individuals to work in brief, concentrated bursts, which ultimately leads to increased efficiency. When aware of the time constraint, individuals tend to minimize distractions and concentrate solely on the task, resulting in higher quality work in less time. The structured nature of the technique also aids in setting achievable goals and staying on track, leading to a more productive workflow.

Chapter 3: Effective Time Intervals

3.1 Customization and Adaptation

While the traditional Pomodoro duration is 25 minutes, the technique is highly adaptable to suit individual preferences and work requirements. Some individuals may find it beneficial to adjust the intervals based on their attention span or the nature of the tasks at hand. By experimenting with different durations, individuals can identify the intervals that yield the highest productivity for them.

3.2 Collaboration and Interruptions

In certain work settings, such as collaborative projects or customer service roles, the Pomodoro Technique can be challenging to implement due to frequent interruptions. However, with a few adjustments, it remains possible to adapt the technique even in such scenarios. For instance, individuals can consider shorter Pomodoro intervals to accommodate interruptions or communicate with colleagues about the need for focused work during specific intervals.

Chapter 4: Optimizing the Pomodoro Technique

4.1 Maximizing Breaks

Although the focus of the Pomodoro Technique primarily revolves around work intervals, the importance of breaks should not be underestimated. Short rest periods between Pomodoros enable individuals to recharge their energy levels, consolidate information, and prevent mental strain. Making the most of these breaks by engaging in activities unrelated to work, such as stretching, deep breathing, or going for a short walk, can have a significant positive impact on productivity.

4.2 Combining with Other Techniques

While the Pomodoro Technique offers numerous advantages, it may not be suitable for all situations or individuals. However, it can be effectively combined with other time management strategies to create a personalized approach. For example, incorporating prioritization techniques, such as the Eisenhower Matrix or the Pareto Principle, can help individuals identify tasks deserving of initial focus during Pomodoros.

The Pomodoro Technique and its reliance on time intervals have proven to be an invaluable tool for improving productivity and managing time effectively. By breaking work into manageable chunks and emphasizing focused intervals, individuals can harness their concentration, overcome procrastination, and achieve increased efficiency. With its adaptability and potential for customization, the technique can be easily tailored to fit the needs and preferences of various individuals. Incorporating breaks and combining the technique with other time management strategies further enhances its effectiveness. By implementing the Pomodoro Technique and embracing time intervals, everyone can unlock their true potential and accomplish more in less time.

Temporal Task Batching

In today's fast-paced and ever-demanding world, time is a precious commodity. As individuals and organizations strive to do more with less, the need for efficient time management becomes increasingly vital. One technique that has gained prominence in recent years is temporal task batching. This chapter sets out to explore the concept of temporal task batching, its benefits, and how it can be effectively implemented to enhance both personal and professional productivity.

Understanding Temporal Task Batching:

Temporal task batching, often referred to as time blocking, is a time management strategy that involves grouping similar tasks together and dedicating specific time slots to accomplish them. Instead of tackling tasks as they come, this approach emphasizes organization and prioritization to increase efficiency and effectiveness. By focusing on one task category at a time, individuals can eliminate distractions and fully immerse themselves in the allotted activity.

The Benefits of Temporal Task Batching:

Implementing temporal task batching brings a multitude of advantages, both cognitively and practically. By providing structure and routine, it helps individuals gain a sense of control over their time and reduces decision fatigue. Additionally, this technique promotes better focus and concentration, leading to increased productivity and higher quality output. Let's delve into the three primary benefits of temporal task batching in more detail.

1. Improved Time Management:

The essence of effective time management lies in understanding the value of each moment and allocating it appropriately. Temporal task batching allows individuals to allocate dedicated time blocks for specific activities, ensuring that important tasks are completed in a timely manner. Rather than frantically switching between unrelated tasks, individuals can concentrate on one category at a time, achieving deep focus and maximizing their work output. As a result, deadlines are met, and work-related stress is significantly reduced.

2. Enhanced Concentration:

In today's digital age, distractions are ubiquitous, posing a constant threat to focus and productivity. Temporal task batching serves as a shield against such distractions, enabling individuals to immerse themselves fully in a singular task. By blocking out unnecessary interruptions during dedicated time slots, individuals can harness their mental energy, enabling them to tackle complex and intellectually demanding tasks more effectively. This heightened concentration leads to improved decision-making, problem-solving, and creativity.

3. Stress Reduction and Well-being:

The ability to manage time effectively is closely related to overall mental well-being. Temporal task batching helps create a healthy work-life balance by dividing one's time into manageable chunks. By allocating time for personal activities, relaxation, and self-care, individuals can prevent burnout and maintain a sustainable pace. Additionally, this time management technique allows for more effective prioritization, reducing the feeling of overwhelm caused by approaching deadlines and mounting to-do lists.

Implementing Temporal Task Batching:

To successfully implement temporal task batching, it is crucial to follow a systematic approach. Let's consider the steps involved in effectively organizing and planning one's time using this technique.

Step 1: Task Categorization:

Begin by categorizing tasks based on their nature, priority, and dependencies. Grouping similar tasks together will facilitate smoother transitions between activities.

Step 2: Determining Time Blocks:

Allocate dedicated time slots for each task category, making sure to consider the complexity, energy required, and urgency of each task. Aim for a balance that suits your personal style and preferences.

Step 3: Scheduling and Prioritization:

Create a detailed schedule, assigning specific tasks to their respective time blocks. Prioritize tasks based on deadlines, importance, and impact. Flexibility is key here, as occasional adjustments may be necessary to accommodate changing needs.

Step 4: Eliminating Distractions:

During dedicated time blocks, eliminate or minimize potential distractions. Put your phone on silent, close unnecessary tabs or applications on your computer, and communicate your unavailability to colleagues or family members. This intentional focus will boost productivity and prevent external disruptions.

Step 5: Regular Breaks and Reevaluation:

Integrate periodic breaks into your schedule to maintain mental freshness. Remember, proper time management is not about working non-stop; it's about strategic allocation of both focused work time and rejuvenating breaks. Regularly evaluate your schedule to identify potential areas for improvement, allowing for continuous learning and optimization.

Best Practices for Temporal Task Batching:

While the concept of temporal task batching is relatively simple, implementing it effectively requires commitment and discipline. Here are some best practices to help you make the most of this productivity-enhancing technique:

1. Start with Simple Batches: Ease into temporal task batching by beginning with simple task groups. As you gain confidence and experience, gradually expand the number and complexity of tasks within each batch.

2. Account for Energy Levels: Consider your natural energy patterns and identify the best times of day for different types of tasks. Allocate mentally demanding and creative activities to periods when your energy is high, and routine or administrative tasks to periods when you naturally experience lower energy levels.

3. Manage Interruptions: Interruptions can disrupt your workflow and hinder productivity, even with task batching. If an urgent matter arises during a dedicated block, evaluate its importance and whether it can be rescheduled. If necessary, shift your schedule accordingly and maintain your focus once the interruption is handled.

4. Leverage Technology: Explore productivity tools and time management apps that can assist in planning and scheduling tasks. Utilizing automation and reminders will help you stay on track and maintain consistency in your temporal task batching practice.

5. Stay Committed and Iterative: Embrace temporal task batching as a long-term habit and remain committed to the process. Like any new skill, it may take time to refine and adapt your approach. Regularly assess your results, seek feedback, and make iterative

improvements to your planning and execution.

Temporal task batching is a valuable strategy that can transform the way individuals manage their time, enabling them to achieve higher productivity and a healthier work-life balance. By organizing tasks into focused time blocks, setting priorities, and minimizing distractions, individuals can harness their mental energy, accomplish more in less time, and experience reduced stress levels. The implementation of this technique requires discipline, adaptability, and a commitment to continuous improvement. Ultimately, with the right approach and dedication, temporal task batching can empower individuals and organizations to unlock their full potential.

The Kanban System and Flow State Timing

In today's fast-paced business world, organizations constantly strive to find efficient ways to manage their work processes. Among the various techniques available, the Kanban system has gained popularity for its simplicity, flexibility, and ability to increase productivity. Moreover, combining the Kanban system with the concept of flow state timing presents an intriguing approach to optimizing work performance. In this chapter, we will explore the principles and benefits of the Kanban system, and how incorporating flow state timing into its implementation can greatly enhance productivity and untap human potential.

Understanding the Kanban System:

The Kanban system originated from the Toyota Production System (TPS) in Japan and was initially used to manage manufacturing operations. It later evolved into a broad project management framework applicable to various industries. The word "Kanban" translates to "visual signal," emphasizing the system's visual nature.

Kanban revolves around the principle of pull-based work management, emphasizing the need to minimize waste by aligning work processes with actual demand. The system employs visual cues, typically represented by cards on a board, to track and visualize work items throughout different stages of a process. Each stage of the workflow represents a column on the Kanban board, enabling teams to visualize their progress and identify bottlenecks or areas that require attention.

Implementing the Kanban System:

1. Mapping the Workflow: The first step in implementing the Kanban system is to map out the workflow. By identifying the various stages a project goes through from start to finish, teams gain a clear understanding of the entire process. This visualization provides insight into the interdependencies between tasks and helps identify potential areas for improvement.

2. Establishing Work-in-Progress (WIP) Limits: Kanban allows teams to enforce WIP limits for each stage of the workflow, preventing overburdening and ensuring a smooth flow of work. By limiting the number of items that can be in progress at any given time, teams can better focus on completing tasks, reduce context switching, and increase collaboration.

3. Visualizing the Workflow: Using a visual Kanban board, teams can track the progress of individual tasks, ensuring transparency and promoting better communication. The board provides an at-a-glance view of the entire workflow and a shared understanding among team members, accelerating decision-making, and improving overall productivity.

4. Monitoring Flow and Continuous Improvement: The Kanban system allows teams to monitor the flow of work continuously. By measuring cycle times, lead times, and tracking other relevant metrics, organizations gain valuable insights into their work processes. This data-driven approach enables teams to identify areas of improvement, make informed decisions, and enhance overall efficiency.

Introducing Flow State Timing:

Flow state, coined by psychologist Mihaly Csikszentmihalyi, refers to a mental state of complete immersion in an activity, where individuals experience deep focus, high productivity, and a sense of timelessness. When combined with the Kanban system, flow state timing provides a unique opportunity to unlock a higher level of performance by leveraging individual focus and concentration.

Flow state timing emphasizes the importance of allocating dedicated time blocks for focused work, minimizing distractions, and providing an environment conducive to profound concentration. By encouraging individuals to work in uninterrupted intervals, typically ranging from 30 minutes to two hours, flow state timing allows individuals to delve into their tasks with heightened efficiency and creativity.

Benefits of Combining Kanban and Flow State Timing:

The integration of the Kanban system and flow state timing offers several key benefits, transforming work management practices and unlocking untapped productivity potential:

1. Enhanced Focus and Engagement: By incorporating flow state timing into the Kanban system, individuals can experience longer and more profound periods of focus, thereby boosting productivity and overall engagement. The clear visualization of work stages in Kanban, coupled with the immersive nature of flow state timing, helps individuals eliminate distractions and stay fully engaged with their tasks.

2. Reduced Multi-tasking and Context Switching: The Kanban system, with its WIP limits, enables teams to focus on a limited number of tasks at a time. Flow state timing further enhances this focus by eliminating the need for frequent context switching, promoting sustained attention to each task and minimizing cognitive load. This, in turn, leads to higher quality outcomes and reduced time wasted on shifting between different responsibilities.

3. Increased Collaboration and Cohesion: The visual nature of the Kanban system fosters transparency, enabling team members to easily track the progress of tasks and identify bottlenecks. Flow state timing complements this by encouraging synchrony, as team members synchronize their focus and dedicated work intervals. This synchronized approach enhances collaboration, fostering a shared sense of purpose and collective progress.

4. Improved Work Satisfaction and Well-being: The combination of the Kanban system and flow state timing promotes a healthy work-life balance and reduces burnout. By providing clear boundaries for focused work, individuals can attain a sense of accomplishment, while also ensuring ample time for breaks and personal activities. This balance contributes to higher job satisfaction, increased motivation, and improved overall well-being.

The Kanban system, coupled with the concept of flow state timing, offers a powerful approach to work management and improved productivity. By visualizing and optimizing workflows, setting WIP limits, and integrating focused work intervals, organizations can unlock remarkable outcomes and tap into the full potential of their teams. Remember, mastering the art of flow state timing is a journey of continuous learning, experimentation, and adaptation. Embrace this dynamic approach to work management, and witness the remarkable transformation it brings to your organization's productivity and overall success.

Chapter 4: Mental and Emotional States in Time Management

In our fast-paced world, effective time management has become crucial for success in both personal and professional lives. Managing our time efficiently allows us to accomplish tasks, meet deadlines, and maintain a healthy work-life balance. While there are various strategies and techniques to master time management, we often overlook the significant role that our mental and emotional states play in this process. This chapter aims to delve into the importance of our mental and emotional well-being while exploring practical ways to enhance these aspects for optimal time management.

Understanding Mental States

Our mental state refers to the overall quality and function of our mind at any given moment. It encompasses our focus, concentration, cognitive abilities, memory, and creativity, among other aspects. A positive mental state is essential for effective time management since it promotes clarity of thought, reduces distractions, and enhances productivity.

One significant factor that influences our mental state is our level of stress. When we experience high levels of stress, our ability to focus diminishes, rendering time management difficult. Therefore, it is crucial to find healthy ways to cope with and manage stress. Engaging in activities such as exercise, meditation, or pursuing hobbies not only reduces stress but also improves mental clarity and concentration.

Another essential element of our mental state is our energy levels. A tired and fatigued mind cannot efficiently manage time. Therefore, it is crucial to prioritize sleep and ensure we get adequate rest to sustain mental stamina throughout our daily routines. Additionally, maintaining a balanced diet and staying hydrated contributes to our mental well-being, increasing our cognitive abilities and allowing for effective time management.

Emotional States and Time Management

Our emotional state profoundly affects our ability to manage time effectively. Emotions such as happiness, motivation, and enthusiasm fuel our productivity, while negative emotions like frustration, anger, or anxiety hinder our time management endeavors. Therefore, maintaining positive emotional states is crucial to boost productivity and accomplish tasks efficiently.

To foster positive emotions, it is vital to create an environment that promotes emotional well-being. This can include engaging in activities that bring joy and fulfillment, surrounding ourselves with positive and supportive individuals, and practicing gratitude. Additionally, managing our workload and setting realistic goals helps to minimize stress and prevent feelings of being overwhelmed, thereby enabling more positive emotional states in our daily lives.

Cultivating emotional intelligence is another essential aspect of effective time management. Emotionally intelligent individuals possess the ability to recognize and regulate their own emotions while empathizing with others. By enhancing emotional intelligence, we become more self-aware, enabling us to identify and manage emotions that can be obstacles to effective time management. Additionally, empathizing with others allows for better understanding and cooperation, leading to improved teamwork and overall efficiency.

Practical Strategies for Mental and Emotional Enhancement

Now that we understand the pivotal role of mental and emotional states in time management, let's explore some practical strategies to enhance these aspects.

1. Mindfulness and meditation: Incorporating mindfulness and meditation practices into our daily routine can improve our mental state by increasing focus, reducing stress, and promoting clarity of

thought.

2. Prioritizing self-care: Carving out time for self-care activities such as exercise, hobbies, or spending time with loved ones replenishes our emotional well-being, leading to increased productivity when managing time.

3. Effective stress management: Implementing stress management techniques, such as deep breathing exercises, social support systems, and time for relaxation, aids in maintaining a positive mental and emotional state.

4. Time-blocking: Allocating specific time slots for different tasks and activities helps to streamline our focus and prevent distractions, resulting in enhanced mental clarity and improved time management.

5. Setting achievable goals: Establishing realistic goals allows for a sense of accomplishment, reducing feelings of overwhelm and promoting positive emotional states. Breaking larger tasks into smaller, more manageable ones aids in creating a structured approach to time management.

6. Regular breaks: Incorporating short breaks throughout our workday helps to recharge our mental state, allowing us to maintain focus and productivity over more extended periods. Utilizing these

breaks for physical activity or engaging in relaxation techniques often proves especially beneficial for mental and emotional enhancement.

The significance of mental and emotional states in time management cannot be overstated. By prioritizing our mental and emotional well-being, we create an optimal environment for effective time management. Recognizing the impact of stress, energy levels, positive emotions, and emotional intelligence helps us establish practical strategies to enhance these areas. Through mindfulness, self-care, stress management, effective goal-setting, and regular breaks, we can improve our mental and emotional states, empowering us to manage time more efficiently. By incorporating these strategies into our lives, we can unlock our true productivity potential and achieve a more balanced and fulfilling life.

Mindfulness in Temporal Mastery

In our fast-paced and ever-evolving world, it can often feel like time passes by in the blink of an eye. The relentless demands of modern life can leave us feeling overwhelmed, disconnected, and trapped in a perpetual cycle of busyness. However, the ancient practice of mindfulness offers a way to navigate these challenges and regain control over our relationship with time. In this chapter, we will explore the concept of mindfulness in the context of temporal mastery, providing practical tools and insights to help you cultivate a more conscious and fulfilling approach to time management.

Understanding Temporal Mastery

Before delving into the role of mindfulness in temporal mastery, it is important to first establish a clear understanding of this concept. Temporal mastery refers to the ability to skillfully manage our time, making conscious choices about how we allocate, utilize, and appreciate it. It is not about attempting to control time itself, but rather about gaining mastery over our own actions and attitudes in relation to time.

1. The Illusion of Time

To fully appreciate the significance of temporal mastery, we must first acknowledge the illusory nature of time. Time is a human construct, a mental framework that helps us organize and make sense of the world around us. However, it is important to recognize that time, in its essence, is fluid and subjective. Each individual experiences time differently, influenced by factors such as perception, attention, and emotional state.

2. The Pitfalls of Temporal Disempowerment

In today's fast-paced society, many individuals find themselves at the mercy of time, perceiving it as an external force that governs their lives. This temporal disempowerment not only leads to stress and anxiety but can also perpetuate a sense of helplessness and disconnection from the present moment. Without mindful awareness, we may fall into the trap of constantly chasing after future goals or dwelling on past regrets, losing sight of the only moment we truly have - the present.

The Role of Mindfulness

Mindfulness, originating from ancient Buddhist practices, has gained significant attention in recent years due to its ability to cultivate heightened awareness and presence. When applied to temporal mastery, mindfulness offers a powerful tool for reconnecting with the present moment, developing a sense of agency over time, and fostering a more fulfilling experience of life itself.

1. Cultivating Present-Moment Awareness

At its core, mindfulness involves intentionally paying attention to the present moment without judgment. By practicing mindfulness, we can free ourselves from the mental clutter and distractions that often derail our attempts to manage time effectively. By bringing our attention to the here and now, we become more attuned to the passage of time and better equipped to make intentional choices regarding how we spend it.

2. Embracing the Power of Choice

Mindfulness empowers us to recognize that each moment presents an opportunity for choice. By cultivating awareness, we can identify and break free from habitual patterns that rob us of our time and energy. We can make conscious decisions about our priorities, setting intentions that align with our values and aspirations. Mindful time management involves discerning between tasks that truly deserve our attention and those that can be let go or delegated to create more space for what truly matters.

3. Taming the Time-Vampire Mind

Our minds have a tendency to wander, constantly oscillating between past regrets and future worries. These ruminations not only steal our attention but also distort our perception of time. Through regular mindfulness practice, we can train our minds to let go of unhelpful thoughts and bring our focus back to the present. By anchoring ourselves in the here and now, we enhance our ability to make conscious choices that align with our temporal goals.

4. Savoring the Gifts of Time

Mindfulness teaches us to appreciate the beauty and richness of each moment, no matter how fleeting. By cultivating a sense of gratitude and awe for the passage of time, we can shift our perspective from one of scarcity to one of abundance. This shift allows us to derive greater joy and fulfillment from both ordinary and extraordinary moments, deepening our connection with ourselves, others, and the world around us.

Practical Strategies for Mindful Time Management

Now that we have explored the theoretical foundations of mindfulness in temporal mastery, let's delve into some practical strategies that can be applied to our daily lives. These strategies provide a starting point for cultivating a more mindful approach to time management and ultimately achieving temporal mastery.

1. Establish a Daily Mindfulness Practice

Begin by setting aside dedicated time each day to engage in formal mindfulness practice. Whether it's through meditation, mindful movement, or breath awareness, this practice serves as the foundation for developing present-moment awareness. Start with just a few minutes and gradually increase the duration as your practice deepens.

2. Develop a Time Audit

Conducting a thorough assessment of how you currently spend your time is an essential step towards mindful time management. Take a week or two to log your activities, noting the time spent on each task and how it aligns with your values and aspirations. This audit will provide valuable insights into how you can make more conscious choices about time allocation.

3. Prioritize Meaningful Activities

Once you have identified your priorities and values, make a conscious effort to allocate time to activities that align with them. This may involve saying no to non-essential tasks, delegating responsibilities when possible, or reevaluating commitments that no longer serve you. By focusing on what truly matters, you create space for deeper engagement and fulfillment.

4. Practice Single-Tasking

In a world that often glorifies multitasking, practicing single-tasking can be transformative. By focusing our full attention on one task at a time, we enhance our presence and effectiveness, reducing distractions and improving overall productivity. Remember, quality trumps quantity when it comes to mindful time management.

5. Create Mindful Transitions

Transitions between tasks and activities can be prime opportunities for cultivating mindfulness. Instead of rushing from one task to the next, take a moment to pause, breathe, and consciously shift your attention. By bringing a sense of presence to these transitions, you set a positive tone for the task ahead, enhancing focus and reducing stress.

6. Embrace Moments of Stillness

In the hustle and bustle of modern life, it's easy to neglect the importance of rest and rejuvenation. Building moments of stillness into your day, whether through regular breaks, mindful walks, or simply taking a few deep breaths, allows you to recharge and realign your focus. Remember, true mastery of time requires finding balance between activity and rest.

Mindfulness in temporal mastery offers a pathway towards reclaiming our relationship with time. By cultivating awareness, intentionality, and presence, we can transform our experience of time from one of hurriedness and disconnection to one of fulfillment and agency.

As you apply the principles and strategies discussed in this chapter to your own life, may you find a deep sense of mastery over time and a renewed appreciation for the precious moments that make up the tapestry of life.

Emotional Intelligence and Time Perception

Time is a subjective concept that varies from person to person. Some individuals feel that time flies by, while others perceive it as moving at a sluggish pace. This chapter explores the intriguing connection between emotional intelligence and time perception. Are emotionally intelligent individuals more likely to accurately gauge the passage of time? How do emotions influence our perception of time? Through a series of studies and research findings, we aim to shed light on this fascinating relationship.

Defining Emotional Intelligence

Emotional intelligence (EI) refers to the ability to recognize, understand, and manage our emotions effectively. It encompasses various skills such as emotional awareness, self-regulation, empathy, and social skills. Researchers have identified four key components of emotional intelligence: self-awareness, self-management, social awareness, and relationship management. These components collectively contribute to an individual's overall emotional well-being and interpersonal relationships.

Perception of Time

Before delving into the relationship between emotional intelligence and time perception, it is crucial to understand the concept of time perception itself. Time perception refers to the subjective experience of the passage of time. It involves our ability to estimate durations, intervals, and the perception of the speed at which time is passing.

It is no secret that our perception of time is malleable and can be influenced by various factors, including our emotional state. Time can appear to slow down or speed up depending on our circumstances and emotions at any given moment. For instance, in situations of extreme danger or excitement, time often feels as though it is moving in slow motion, while in periods of boredom or sadness, time can seemingly crawl by.

Emotional Intelligence and Time Estimation

One area of interest within the realm of emotional intelligence and time perception research is the estimation of time intervals. Several studies have demonstrated that individuals with high emotional intelligence tend to exhibit more accurate time estimations compared to those with lower emotional intelligence.

A study conducted by Phillips, Tunstall, and Murray (2010) explored the relationship between emotional intelligence and time estimation in a laboratory setting. Participants were administered a widely used emotional intelligence questionnaire and subsequently asked to estimate the duration of several time intervals. The results indicated a significant positive correlation between emotional intelligence and accurate time estimations, suggesting that individuals with higher emotional intelligence possess a more precise perception of time.

This finding can be attributed to the self-awareness component of emotional intelligence. Individuals who are highly self-aware are more attuned to their emotions and bodily sensations. Consequently, they are more likely to accurately gauge the passage of time as they are tuned into their internal clock mechanisms.

Emotional State and Time Perception

While emotional intelligence may enhance our ability to estimate time accurately, our emotional state can also influence the subjective experience of time. Positive emotions, such as joy and excitement, often lead to an overestimation of time, making it appear longer than it actually is. On the contrary, negative emotions, such as sadness or pain, tend to make time feel shorter, resulting in an underestimation of duration.

Studies have revealed that people tend to be more accurate in their time estimations when they are in a neutral emotional state rather than experiencing extreme emotions. This suggests that emotional arousal, whether positive or negative, can distort our perception of time. It is important to note that the intensity of emotions also plays a role in time distortion. Heightened emotional states, whether positive or negative, amplify the effect on time perception.

Integrating Emotional Intelligence with Time Management

Time management is a crucial aspect of our daily lives, impacting our productivity, stress levels, and overall well-being. Emotional intelligence can play a significant role in optimizing our time management skills.

When we are emotionally intelligent, we can effectively prioritize tasks, set realistic goals, and remain resilient in the face of setbacks. Additionally, emotional intelligence allows us to understand our personal energy patterns, identifying periods of peak productivity and moments that require relaxation or rejuvenation. By aligning our activities with our emotional state, we can maximize our efficiency and achieve a healthy work-life balance.

Furthermore, emotional intelligence enables us to recognize and respond to the emotions of others, fostering better collaboration and teamwork. This, in turn, can streamline processes and reduce time wastage in interpersonal interactions.

As we have explored in this chapter, emotional intelligence and time perception are intricately linked. Individuals with higher emotional intelligence tend to possess a more accurate perception of time, while emotional states can distort our temporal experiences. Moreover, integrating emotional intelligence into our time management strategies enables us to optimize productivity and well-being.

Understanding the intricate relationship between emotional intelligence and time perception can have far-reaching implications in various domains, such as education, healthcare, and personal development. By harnessing the power of emotional intelligence and efficiently managing our time, we can navigate the complexities of life more effectively, leading to enhanced overall satisfaction and success.

Reducing Time Anxiety

Tick-tock, tick-tock. Time. It is an elusive and intriguing entity that consumes our every moment. Often, we find ourselves fixating on its incessant ticking, letting anxiety grip our minds and hearts. In today's fast-paced world, where everything operates on the premise of efficiency, it is no wonder that we experience a prevailing sense of time anxiety.

But what is time anxiety? It is that nagging feeling that we are never doing enough, that we are always running behind, and that the precious minutes are slipping through our fingers like grains of sand. Fueled by the incessant pressures of work, technology, and societal expectations, this anxiety haunts us, leaving us feeling overwhelmed and disconnected from the richness of life.

We will delve into the depths of time anxiety, its causes, and how it can impact our overall well-being. By understanding the roots of this crippling anxiety, we can embark on a journey toward liberation and find harmony in the present.

The Acceleration of Modern Life

As the world hurtles toward greater technological advancements, our lives become increasingly cluttered with distractions. From smartphones to social media platforms, we find ourselves caught in a whirlwind of notifications, deadlines, and instantaneous expectations. Our attention is fragmented, and every moment is consumed by the need to keep up with the tremendous speed of modern life.

We will explore the acceleration of modern life and its role in fueling time anxiety. We will delve into the pressures of multitasking, productivity cults, and the constant need to be "on." By understanding the social and cultural factors contributing to our anxious relationship with time, we can take the first steps toward breaking free from its constraints.

The Mind-Traps of Regret and Foresight

Regret and foresight are two powerful mental constructs that perpetuate our time anxiety. Whether it is regretting missed opportunities or worrying incessantly about the future, these mind-traps anchor us to an escalating cycle of anxiety and dissatisfaction. The past and the future become lenses through which we view ourselves and our world, leading us to neglect the present and the beauty it holds.

We will unveil the intricacies of regret and foresight, exploring their origins and understanding how they intertwine with our perception of time. By learning to navigate these mental constructs and refocus our awareness on the present, we can find peace and contentment in the here and now.

The Illusion of Time Management

Time management—the holy grail of our modern society. We are constantly inundated with tips, tricks, and hacks promising to help us seize every second. However, as we fall deeper into the rabbit hole of time management, we often find ourselves feeling even more overwhelmed and anxious, trapped in a never-ending pursuit of productivity.

We will debunk the myth of time management and explore alternative approaches that prioritize mindfulness and intentionality. We will delve into the philosophy of slow living, the power of prioritization, and the art of saying no. By shifting our focus from managing time to managing ourselves, we can reclaim control over our lives and reduce time anxiety.

Embracing the Power of Mindfulness

In a world marred by the obsession to always be ahead, the true antidote lies in the practice of mindfulness. Mindfulness is the art of being fully present, appreciating the current moment without judgment or attachment. It is a tool that allows us to escape the clutches of time anxiety and connect with the depth and richness of every experience.

We will unravel the profound benefits of mindfulness and explore practical techniques that can be integrated into our daily lives. From meditation to mindful eating, we will learn to embrace the power of the present moment, fostering a sense of gratitude and contentment that transcends the hurried pace of our world.

Nurturing Balance and Connection

As we navigate our way through the labyrinth of time anxiety, we often lose sight of an essential aspect of our lives—balance. The pursuit of balance involves harmonizing our personal and professional spheres, as well as cultivating meaningful relationships and nurturing our physical and mental well-being.

We will explore strategies for finding balance and establishing healthy boundaries that protect our time and energy. We will delve into the importance of self-care, the art of unplugging, and the significance of fostering authentic connections with loved ones. By prioritizing balance and connection, we can cultivate a sense of fulfillment and reduce the grip of time anxiety in our lives.

Stepping into the Present

The Tick-tock, tick-tock that once instilled fear and anxiety will no longer dictate our lives. Armed with a deeper understanding of time anxiety, the societal factors that fuel it, and the tools necessary to counteract it, we are ready to embrace the present and unlock a balanced life.

Cultivating a Growth Mindset for Time Efficiency

In today's fast-paced world, time efficiency has become crucial for success in both personal and professional spheres. However, many individuals find themselves struggling to make the best use of their time, often feeling overwhelmed and defeated. The key to overcoming this challenge lies in cultivating a growth mindset – a mindset that embraces challenges, learns from failures, and believes in the power of effort. In this chapter, we will explore how adopting a growth mindset can enhance time efficiency, helping you become more productive, organized, and focused in your daily life.

The Power of Mindset:

Before delving into the specifics of time efficiency, it is essential to understand the impact of mindset on our overall well-being and success. Mindset refers to the collection of beliefs and attitudes we hold about ourselves, others, and the world around us. Psychologist Carol Dweck introduced the concept of fixed and growth mindsets. A fixed mindset assumes that talents and abilities are fixed traits, while a growth mindset sees them as qualities that can be developed through dedication and effort.

Individuals with a fixed mindset often view challenges as threats and tend to give up easily when faced with obstacles. Conversely, those with a growth mindset embrace challenges, persevere through setbacks, and see failures as valuable learning experiences. By adopting a growth mindset, you can transform your approach to time management and unlock your full potential.

Embracing Challenges:

One of the fundamental aspects of a growth mindset is the willingness to embrace challenges. Rather than shying away from difficult tasks, individuals who cultivate a growth mindset understand that challenges provide an opportunity for growth and learning. When it comes to time efficiency, this mindset shift allows you to approach your daily tasks and responsibilities with enthusiasm and curiosity.

Instead of feeling overwhelmed by a looming deadline, consider it a chance to stretch your capabilities and develop effective time management strategies. Embracing challenges also means seeking out new opportunities to expand your skills and knowledge. This could involve taking on projects outside of your comfort zone or acquiring new time-saving techniques and tools. By reframing challenges as growth opportunities, you will develop the resilience and tenacity necessary for optimum time efficiency.

Learning from Failures:

Failures often serve as a stumbling block for many individuals, causing stress, frustration, and a loss of time. However, with a growth mindset, failures are seen as valuable stepping stones on the path to success. Embracing failures and learning from them is essential for cultivating a growth mindset and improving time efficiency.

When faced with a setback, take the time to reflect on what went wrong and why. Learning from your mistakes allows for continuous improvement and a more efficient use of your time in the future. By analyzing the factors that led to the failure, you can adjust your time management strategies, identify areas of weakness, and develop new skills. This growth-oriented approach ensures that setbacks become opportunities for growth rather than roadblocks to success.

Believing in the Power of Effort:
Individuals with a growth mindset firmly believe in the power of effort and understand that true success is a result of hard work and dedication. When striving for time efficiency, this belief becomes a driving force, motivating you to invest your efforts into organizing and optimizing your daily routines.

Recognize that time efficiency is not about finding shortcuts or quick fixes but about implementing sustainable habits and efficient workflows. By dedicating time and effort to develop a well-structured schedule, prioritizing tasks, and eliminating distractions, you will maximize your productivity and create more time for activities that truly matter. A growth mindset allows you to approach every task with the mentality that effort will lead to improvement and overall time efficiency.

Developing Resilience:

In the pursuit of time efficiency, it is crucial to develop resilience to bounce back from setbacks and challenges. A growth mindset fosters resilience by cultivating a positive attitude towards failures and recognizing that setbacks are temporary obstacles on the path to success.

When facing time-related challenges, such as unexpected interruptions or delays, a resilient mindset helps you adapt and find alternative solutions. Rather than allowing these disruptions to derail your progress, a growth mindset encourages you to remain focused, adaptable, and proactive in finding ways to regain control over your time. Resilience allows you to persevere and maintain a steady course towards achieving your goals while making the most efficient use of available time.

Cultivating a growth mindset is a transformative journey that can significantly enhance your time efficiency. By embracing challenges, learning from failures, believing in the power of effort, and developing resilience, you will unlock your full potential, making the best use of your time to achieve personal and professional success. Remember, adopting a growth mindset is a lifelong process that requires consistent effort and practice. By nurturing this mindset, you will not only boost your time efficiency but also foster personal growth, leading to a more fulfilling and accomplished life.

Chapter 5: Temporal Habits of Highly Effective Individuals

In our fast-paced society, time management has become a crucial skill for individuals striving for productivity and success. Successful individuals understand that how they organize their time and utilize it effectively can greatly impact all aspects of their life. In this chapter, we will delve into the temporal habits of highly effective individuals, examining their strategies, routines, and mindset that allow them to optimize their time. By adopting and implementing these proven techniques, you too can enhance your productivity and achieve your goals.

1. The Power of Prioritization:

Highly effective individuals are masters of prioritization. They recognize that not all tasks carry the same level of importance and impact. They invest time upfront in analyzing and determining which tasks align with their long-term goals. By differentiating between urgent and important tasks, they create a roadmap for their daily activities. They prioritize significant, high-impact tasks and tackle them first, ensuring progress towards their ultimate objectives.

2. Structured Scheduling:

A key trait of highly effective individuals is their commitment to structured scheduling. They understand that an organized and well-planned schedule is paramount for productivity. They allocate specific blocks of time for different types of activities, such as focused work, meetings, breaks, and personal time. By creating a comprehensive schedule, they establish a framework that minimizes time wasted on decision-making and maximizes the efficiency of their workflow.

3. Time Blocking:

An effective technique leveraged by highly productive individuals is time blocking. It involves dedicating specific time blocks to focused work on a single task without interruptions. By eliminating distractions and solely focusing on one task at a time, they achieve heightened levels of concentration and quality output. Time blocking also allows for better estimation of the time required for completing various tasks, paving the way for more accurate scheduling.

4. The Pomodoro Technique:

The Pomodoro Technique is a popular time management method embraced by highly effective individuals. It involves breaking work into intervals of focused effort, usually 25 minutes, followed by short breaks of around 5 minutes. After completing a set of four intervals, they take a longer break. By working in short sprints, highly effective individuals reduce burnout, maintain productivity, and overcome procrastination.

5. Mindfulness and Mindset Shift:

Highly effective individuals understand the significance of mindfulness and cultivating the right mindset. They prioritize self-reflection, meditation, and other mindfulness practices to develop self-awareness and clarity. By managing their mental state, they can better face challenges, regulate stress, and improve their decision-making abilities. Moreover, they adopt a growth mindset, believing in the power of continuous learning, improvement, and adaptation.

6. Delegation and Outsourcing:

One of the secrets of highly effective individuals lies in their ability to delegate and outsource tasks. They recognize that they cannot do everything on their own and that leveraging the expertise of others is not a sign of weakness, but rather a strategic move. By delegating lower-priority and time-consuming tasks to competent individuals or outsourcing to professionals, they free their time for essential activities that align with their strengths and goals.

7. Minimizing Multitasking:

Contrary to popular belief, highly effective individuals do not pride themselves on multitasking. Instead, they focus on single-tasking, dedicating their full attention to one activity at a time. Research has shown that multitasking can decrease efficiency and lead to more errors due to divided attention. By resisting the temptation to multitask, highly effective individuals maintain a higher level of concentration and produce superior outcomes.

8. Non-Negotiable Downtime:

Highly effective individuals understand the importance of downtime for recharging and maintaining overall well-being. They incorporate non-negotiable downtime into their schedules, ensuring periods of rest and relaxation. Whether it is spending quality time with loved ones, pursuing hobbies, or engaging in physical exercise, they prioritize activities that nurture their mental, emotional, and physical health.

9. Continuous Learning and Skill Development:

A hallmark of highly effective individuals is their commitment to continuous learning and skill development. They recognize that the world is constantly evolving, and to stay ahead, they need to keep expanding their knowledge and acquiring new skills. They set aside dedicated time for reading, attending courses, networking, and staying abreast of industry trends. By investing in their personal and professional growth, they enhance their productivity and adaptability in an ever-changing landscape.

Morning Routines and the Golden Hours

As the sun rises and casts its warm rays upon the earth, a new day begins, full of possibilities and opportunities. The way we start our mornings sets the tone for the rest of the day, making it essential to prioritize our routines during these precious hours. In this chapter, we will delve into the concept of morning routines, exploring their significance and the art of making the most of the "Golden Hours."

The definition of a morning routine may vary from person to person, but at its core, it is a set of activities performed consistently each morning to begin the day on a positive note. Establishing a morning routine offers a myriad of benefits, allowing us to cultivate discipline, clarity, and focus, ultimately enhancing productivity and well-being.

Setting the alarm clock to wake up a bit earlier than usual can work wonders for creating a fulfilling morning routine. This extra time in the morning provides an opportunity to engage in activities that nurture our mind, body, and spirit before the demands of the day take over. Let's now explore some components of an ideal morning routine that can help us seize the Golden Hours.

1. Rising with Gratitude:

To kick-start your morning on a positive note, begin by expressing gratitude for the gift of a new day. Take a moment to reflect on the blessings in your life, whether big or small. Appreciating what we have sets a joyful tone for the rest of the day, cultivating an attitude of abundance and mindfulness.

2. Hydrating the Body:

Dehydration is often an invisible culprit that can leave us feeling sluggish and slow. Upon waking, aim to hydrate your body by consuming a glass of water. For extra benefits, add a slice of lemon or a sprinkle of natural electrolytes to invigorate your senses and re-energize your body.

3. Mindful Movement:

Engaging in gentle exercises, such as yoga, stretching, or a brisk walk, is an excellent way to awaken the body and stimulate blood circulation. Physical activity in the morning boosts energy, releases endorphins, and prepares you for the challenges of the day ahead.

4. A Nourishing Breakfast:

Breakfast is often referred to as the most important meal of the day, and for good reason. It provides the necessary fuel to jumpstart our metabolism and maintain stable blood sugar levels. Choose a nutritious breakfast that includes a balance of whole grains, protein, and fresh fruits or vegetables. Allow yourself time to savor this meal mindfully, feeding not only the body but also the soul.

5. Journaling and Affirmations:

The power of journaling lies in its ability to foster self-reflection, creativity, and emotional well-being. Take a few moments each morning to jot down your thoughts, goals, and aspirations. Additionally, practicing affirmations—positive statements that affirm your abilities and desires—can set the tone for a productive and fulfilling day.

6. Meditation and Mindfulness:

In our fast-paced world, finding moments of peace and stillness is crucial. Integrating meditation into your morning routine allows you to connect with your inner self, reduce stress, and cultivate a calm and focused mindset. By practicing mindfulness, you become more present in each moment and fully appreciate the beauty and opportunities that arise throughout the day.

7. Engaging in Personal Growth:

The mornings offer a serene environment where personal growth activities can flourish. Whether it's reading a few pages of an inspiring book, listening to motivational podcasts, or engaging in personal development exercises, investing time in your personal growth fuels your mind and expands your perspectives.

8. Prioritizing Your Tasks:

Utilizing the Golden Hours to plan and prioritize tasks for the day is an essential step in maintaining focus and productivity. Take a few minutes to review your calendar, set goals, and allocate time for the most important and urgent tasks. By doing so, you will approach the day with a clear roadmap, enabling you to make steady progress towards your objectives.

Embracing morning routines and the Golden Hours requires commitment, but the rewards far outweigh the effort. As we establish a consistent morning routine, it becomes a ritual that nourishes our mind, body, and spirit. These daily habits create a foundation for success and well-being, empowering us to approach each new day with enthusiasm and purpose.

The morning hours offer a precious window of opportunity to set the tone for the rest of the day. By incorporating activities such as expressing gratitude, hydrating, gentle exercises, enjoying a nutritious breakfast, journaling, meditating, and investing in personal growth, we make the most of the Golden Hours. These intentional practices cultivate discipline, clarity, and focus, enabling us to embrace the day with positivity, productivity, and a renewed sense of purpose. So, seize the mornings, embrace your routine, and unlock the full potential of each day.

Scheduled Reflective Breaks

In our modern society, we often find ourselves caught up in the chaos and busyness of daily life. From the moment we wake up until we collapse into bed at night, our days are filled with endless tasks, responsibilities, and distractions. In this fast-paced world, we rarely take the time to pause, think, and reflect on our experiences. However, recent research has highlighted the importance of incorporating scheduled reflective breaks into our lives. These breaks provide us with an opportunity to introspect, gain valuable insights, and cultivate a deeper understanding of ourselves and our surroundings. In this chapter, we will explore the concept of Scheduled Reflective Breaks and the numerous benefits they can bring to our mental, emotional, and physical well-being.

Defining Reflective Breaks

Before delving deeper into the topic, it is essential to understand what we mean by "Reflective Breaks." These breaks are intentional periods of time set aside for the purpose of self-reflection, contemplation, and mindfulness. Unlike mere moments of solitude, Reflective Breaks require us to disconnect from external distractions and direct our attention inwards. They allow us to process our thoughts, emotions, and experiences, enhancing our ability to make meaningful connections and gain valuable insights about ourselves and our lives.

The Importance of Scheduled Reflective Breaks

1. Enhanced Well-being:

Scheduled Reflective Breaks can significantly improve our overall well-being. By taking time to pause and reflect, we create space for self-care, mental rejuvenation, and self-awareness. As we explore our thoughts and emotions, we gain clarity, reduce stress levels, and improve our emotional intelligence. Moreover, Reflective Breaks enable us to identify negative patterns and behaviors, leading to personal growth and a sense of purpose. Ultimately, these breaks support our journey towards a happier and more fulfilling life.

2. Improved Decision-Making:

In our fast-paced and constantly changing world, making decisions can be overwhelming. By incorporating Reflective Breaks into our routines, we give ourselves the opportunity to step back and evaluate our options more thoroughly. Reflective Breaks help us gain perspective, consider various viewpoints, and tap into our intuition. Armed with this newfound insight, we can make more informed decisions, leading to more positive outcomes and decreased decision fatigue.

3. Increased Creativity:

Creativity often flourishes in moments of solitude and stillness. Reflective Breaks provide the ideal opportunity for our minds to wander, allowing new ideas to emerge and take shape. Throughout history, many great thinkers, artists, and writers have attributed significant breakthroughs to moments of reflection and introspection. By scheduling regular Reflective Breaks, we unlock our creativity and tap into the wellspring of inspiration within us.

4. Deepened Relationships:

In our hyper-connected society, the art of authentic communication and deep connection is often lost. Reflective Breaks offer an antidote to this problem by providing the time and space needed to nurture our relationships. By reflecting on our interactions with loved ones, we become more attuned to their needs, desires, and emotions. Additionally, we gain insights into our own communication style and patterns, allowing us to become better listeners, empathizers, and partners. Reflective Breaks cultivate the space for meaningful conversations, fostering stronger bonds and fostering deeper connections.

Practical Strategies for Incorporating Reflective Breaks:

1. Setting Boundaries:

In order to reap the benefits of Reflective Breaks, it is essential to set clear boundaries. Inform your family, friends, and colleagues that you will be unavailable during your designated Reflective Break time. Create a physical or mental shield around this time, ensuring that you are undisturbed and free from distractions.

2. Choose your Environment:

The environment in which you choose to engage in Reflective Breaks can greatly impact their effectiveness. Find a space that promotes relaxation, focus, and introspection. Whether it's a quiet corner of your favorite park, a cozy reading nook, or a dedicated meditation space, it should be a place that resonates with you on a deep level.

3. Mindfulness and Meditation:

Mindfulness and meditation are powerful practices that can deepen the impact of Reflective Breaks. Incorporate mindfulness techniques, such as deep breathing exercises or body scan meditations, into your Reflective Breaks to enhance self-awareness and focus. These practices will keep you grounded and help you connect with your inner self.

4. Journaling:

Record your thoughts and feelings during Reflective Breaks through journaling. Writing provides a tangible outlet for our internal experiences and can serve as a powerful tool for self-reflection. Use your journal to explore your emotions, ponder on life's big questions, or to simply free your mind from clutter. The process of putting your thoughts on paper brings clarity and acts as a catalyst for personal growth and self-discovery.

5. Nature Walks:

Nature has a profound impact on our well-being and clarity of mind. Incorporate nature walks into your Reflective Breaks to reconnect with the natural world. As you immerse yourself in the beauty of nature, let your mind wander and allow the sights, sounds, and scents to invoke a sense of calm and connectedness.

In a world that increasingly demands our attention and consumes our time, it is essential to incorporate Scheduled Reflective Breaks into our lives. By dedicating intentional time to pause, reflect, and recharge, we can improve our overall well-being, enhance our decision-making abilities, boost our creativity, and deepen our relationships. Remember, the benefits of Reflective Breaks go beyond the individual; they ripple outwards, positively impacting our communities and society as a whole. Embrace the power of reflection and let it guide you towards a more fulfilling and enlightened existence.

Rituals for Evening Wind-Down

As the sun sets and casts its golden hues across the sky, it's time to shift gears and prepare for a restful evening ahead. In our modern, fast-paced world, it can be challenging to find moments of tranquility and calm amidst the chaos. However, by embracing the power of rituals, we can create a sense of peace and order that helps us wind down from the day's stresses. In this chapter, we will explore a variety of soothing practices that can guide you towards a restful night's sleep.

1. Unplugging from Technology

In a world where we are constantly bombarded with notifications, messages, and screens, it is crucial to find time to disconnect from the digital world. Begin your evening wind-down ritual by setting aside at least an hour before bedtime to unplug from technology. Turn off your television, put your phone on silent or in another room, and resist the temptation to scroll through social media. This intentional step will help signal to your brain that it's time to relax and unwind.

2. Creating a Cozy Space

Transforming your sleeping space into a haven of comfort is key to setting the right atmosphere for winding down. Consider investing in soft, breathable bedding, plump pillows, and cozy blankets. Dim the lights and customize the aroma of your room through scented candles or essential oils. By creating a peaceful sanctuary, you are inviting relaxation to permeate your surroundings.

3. Gentle Stretching and Yoga

Engaging in gentle stretching or a short yoga practice before bed allows you to release tension, increase flexibility, and promote better sleep. Begin with a few simple stretches such as neck rolls, shoulder stretches, and mindful breathing exercises. Alternatively, you could follow a calming yoga sequence designed specifically for bedtime. Move mindfully and listen to your body as you flow through each pose, allowing the stress of the day to melt away.

4. Journaling and Reflection

Many individuals find solace in the act of journaling, as it provides a space for self-reflection, emotional release, and goal-setting. Take a few moments to sit quietly and write down your thoughts, feelings, and experiences from the day. This practice can help you process any unresolved emotions or worries, allowing you to release them before sleep. Additionally, consider including gratitude in your journaling ritual, expressing appreciation for the positive aspects of your day.

5. Herbal Teas and Soothing Tonics

Sipping on a warm herbal tea or a soothing tonic is a wonderful way to wind down and prepare your body for sleep. Herbal teas such as chamomile, lavender, or valerian root have naturally calming properties that aid in relaxation and promote sleepiness. Alternatively, you can create your own concoctions using ingredients like warm almond milk, honey, turmeric, and ginger. Experiment with different flavors and find the combination that best soothes your senses.

6. Mindful Reading

Engaging in quiet reading before bed can help shift your focus away from the stresses of the day and transport you to a different world. Choose books that inspire tranquility, whether it be a captivating novel, poetry, or spiritual texts. Relax in a comfortable chair or snuggle into bed, allowing yourself to be fully immersed in the words on the pages. Avoid reading on electronic devices, as the blue light emitted can disrupt your sleep patterns.

7. Soothing Soundscapes or Music

Creating a calming soundscape can do wonders for inducing a sense of relaxation and preparing your mind for sleep. Explore a variety of options, such as nature sounds, white noise, soft instrumental music, or guided meditation recordings. Find what resonates with you personally and let the gentle sounds wash over you, soothing any residual tension and filling the space with tranquility.

8. Bedtime Skincare Ritual

Engaging in a nourishing skincare routine before bed not only promotes healthy skin but also serves as a tactile and self-soothing ritual. Begin by removing any makeup or impurities from the day, allowing your skin to breathe freely. Follow this with a gentle cleanse, a hydrating facial mist, and a moisturizer that suits your skin type. Consider adding a facial massage or using facial oils for added relaxation. These simple practices will not only prepare your skin for rest but also signal to your body that it's time to wind down.

Remember that the key to an evening wind-down ritual is creating a space and time that is solely dedicated to nurturing your well-being. Each individual's needs and preferences differ, so feel free to adjust and customize these practices to suit your unique journey towards tranquility. By embracing these rituals for evening wind-down, you will cultivate a sense of peace and balance that carries into your nights, paving the way for restful slumber and renewal.

Periodic Temporal Detoxes

In this fast-paced modern world, where time seems to slip through our fingers like sand, it comes as no surprise that many individuals feel overwhelmed, exhausted, and disconnected. We often find ourselves entangled in the web of daily routines, deadlines, and responsibilities, leaving little time for self-reflection and rejuvenation. Luckily, a solution to this problem lies in the concept of "Periodic Temporal Detoxes" – a practice aimed at restoring balance, enhancing self-awareness, and re-establishing a deep connection with the flow of time. In this chapter, we will explore the significance of periodic temporal detoxes, their benefits, and practical tips on how to incorporate them into our lives.

Understanding Periodic Temporal Detoxes

At its core, the idea of a periodic temporal detox revolves around intentionally stepping away from our hectic schedules and immersing ourselves in a dedicated period of time where we prioritize reflection, relaxation, and personal growth. By taking a step back from the constant rush, we allow ourselves to reset, recharge, and realign our minds, bodies, and souls with the natural rhythms of life.

Benefits of Periodic Temporal Detoxes

1. Restoring Balance: For most of us, our lives are filled with endless to-do lists, commitments, and obligations, leaving little time for rest and rejuvenation. Engaging in periodic temporal detoxes offers an invaluable opportunity to restore balance by prioritizing self-care and reconnecting with our inner selves. This, in turn, can lead to increased productivity, improved mental clarity, and better overall well-being.

2. Enhancing Self-Awareness: In our fast-paced lives, we often find ourselves going through the motions without truly reflecting on our actions and the impact they have on ourselves and others. By detaching ourselves from the constant noise and distractions, we create a conducive environment for self-reflection, introspection, and self-discovery. Periodic temporal detoxes allow us to gain a deeper understanding of our values, desires, and aspirations, enabling us to make more intentional choices in our daily lives.

3. Deep Connection with Time: Time is a fundamental aspect of our existence, yet we often treat it as a mere commodity to be spent without much thought. Engaging in periodic temporal detoxes offers us the chance to cultivate a more meaningful, conscious relationship with time. By slowing down, observing natural phenomena like sunrises and sunsets, or simply being present in the moment, we can develop a heightened appreciation for the ebb and flow of time,

leading to a renewed sense of gratitude and serenity.

Incorporating Periodic Temporal Detoxes into Your Life

1. Establishing Intentions: Before embarking on a temporal detox, it is important to set clear intentions. What do you hope to achieve during this period? Is it to find clarity, restore energy levels, or simply take a break? By defining your intentions, you can tailor your detox experience accordingly and ensure a more fulfilling journey.

2. Designating Time: One of the primary challenges in implementing periodic temporal detoxes is finding dedicated time amidst our busy lives. However, it is crucial to remember that even small pockets of time can reap significant benefits. Whether it's a weekend retreat, a day-long digital detox, or even a few hours carved out of your week, make it a priority to reserve time for yourself and your detox practice.

3. Creating Boundaries: During your detox period, it is essential to establish boundaries to protect your sacred space. Communicate your intentions to friends, family, and colleagues, and kindly request their support in respecting your allotted time. By setting boundaries, you create a safe and uninterrupted environment for your reflection and rejuvenation process.

4. Mindful Practices: Engaging in mindfulness practices can greatly enrich your temporal detox experience. These practices can include meditation, journaling, deep breathing exercises, or spending time in nature. The goal is to cultivate a state of presence and awareness, allowing you to fully immerse yourself in the present moment and

detach from worries and stressors.

5. Disconnecting from Technology: In our fast-paced digital world, constant connectivity can hinder our ability to truly unwind and recharge. Consider incorporating a digital detox into your temporal detox routine. Switch off your devices, refrain from social media, and limit your exposure to screens. Embrace the freedom that comes with disconnecting, giving yourself the space to connect with nature, loved ones, and most importantly, yourself.

6. Exploring Time Mindfully: As you undertake your temporal detox, make a conscious effort to explore time mindfully. Observe the movement of the sun, immerse yourself in the sounds of nature, or engage in slow, deliberate activities such as cooking or gardening. By consciously experiencing the passage of time and finding joy in the present moment, you will deepen your connection to both yourself and the world around you.

Periodic temporal detoxes offer a valuable opportunity to recalibrate, recharge, and re-establish harmony within ourselves. By purposefully setting aside time for self-care, reflection, and mindfulness, we can break free from the cycle of constant busyness and reconnect with the natural flow of time. Incorporating periodic temporal detoxes into our lives allows us to restore balance, enhance self-awareness, and cultivate a profound appreciation for the beauty and significance of time. So, my dear reader, I encourage you to embark on this transformative journey and embark on your very own periodic temporal detox.

Chapter 6: Work-Life Balance in the Age of Hustle

In today's fast-paced and interconnected world, finding a healthy balance between work and personal life has become increasingly challenging. The rapid advancements in technology, coupled with societal pressures and the rise of the hustle culture, have created an environment that often prioritizes productivity and achievement over our overall well-being. In this chapter, we will explore the concept of work-life balance, its significance in the modern era, and strategies for achieving it amidst the hustle and bustle of daily life.

The Changing Landscape of Work:

Before we dive into the intricacies of work-life balance, it is essential to understand how the nature of work has evolved over time. Traditional nine-to-five jobs have gradually been replaced by more flexible work arrangements, such as freelancing, remote work, and gig economy opportunities. While these options offer greater autonomy and freedom, they can also blur the boundaries between work and personal life.

The Rise of the Hustle Culture:

One of the key factors contributing to the erosion of work-life balance is the pervasive hustle culture that has permeated society. Hustle culture refers to the glorification of overwork, constant busyness, and sacrificing personal well-being for professional success. This phenomenon often leads to burnout, chronic stress, and an imbalance in every aspect of our lives.

Understanding Work-Life Balance:

Work-life balance is not a one-size-fits-all concept. It varies for each individual depending on their personal values, priorities, and life circumstances. Achieving work-life balance entails finding harmony between one's career, relationships, health, personal growth, and leisure activities. It is about allocating time and energy to different domains rather than allowing work to consume every aspect of our lives.

Reframing Productivity:

In our quest for work-life balance, it is crucial to redefine productivity. Instead of measuring success solely by the number of hours worked or the volume of tasks completed, we must shift our focus towards the quality of our work and our overall well-being. Productivity should not be synonymous with burnout; it should involve sustainable practices that enhance both our professional and personal lives.

Establishing Boundaries:

Creating clear boundaries is an essential step towards achieving work-life balance. It involves setting limits on the time and energy dedicated to work and ensuring that personal life receives the attention it deserves. This can be challenging, particularly for individuals accustomed to the hustle culture, but establishing boundaries is fundamental to preventing burnout and maintaining a healthy lifestyle.

Managing Time Effectively:

One of the most significant contributors to work-life imbalance is poor time management. Learning how to prioritize tasks, delegate responsibilities, and say no when necessary is vital for ensuring we have adequate time for both work and personal life. By being mindful of how we allocate our time, we can strike a better balance and avoid feeling overwhelmed by an ever-growing to-do list.

Redefining Success:

Society often defines success in terms of professional achievements, but true success goes beyond career accolades. To achieve work-life balance, it is crucial to redefine success on our own terms and align it with our personal values and aspirations. This may involve reflecting on what truly brings us happiness and fulfillment and making conscious decisions to pursue a well-rounded life rather than prioritizing work alone.

Cultivating Mindfulness:

Mindfulness refers to the practice of being fully present in the current moment without judgment. Incorporating mindfulness into our daily lives can help us manage stress, enhance focus, and improve overall well-being. By being aware of our thoughts, emotions, and physical sensations, we can navigate the demands of work and life with more clarity and intention.

Building Support Networks:

Maintaining work-life balance is often challenging when we try to do it alone. Building a strong support network, including family, friends, mentors, and colleagues, is crucial for finding support, guidance, and encouragement. Surrounding ourselves with individuals who prioritize work-life balance can influence our own behaviors and help us stay accountable to our goals.

The Importance of Self-Care:

Self-care is a fundamental aspect of achieving work-life balance. It involves taking deliberate actions to nurture our physical, mental, and emotional well-being. Engaging in activities that bring us joy, practicing relaxation techniques, prioritizing sleep, and fostering healthy habits are all essential components of self-care. By prioritizing our own needs, we can recharge, reduce stress, and maintain a healthier work-life balance.

Work-life balance is an ongoing journey that requires continuous effort and self-reflection. With the rapid pace of modern life, it has become increasingly crucial to prioritize our well-being and find harmony between our personal and professional lives. By implementing the strategies and practices discussed in this chapter, we can cultivate a healthier work-life balance in the age of hustle, leading to greater happiness, fulfillment, and overall success in all aspects of our lives.

The Truth Behind 24/7 Productivity

In this fast-paced and hyper-connected world, it seems like everyone is striving for round-the-clock productivity. The concept of being productive 24/7 has become a badge of honor, a symbol of success in our society. But is it truly feasible, or is it just a mirage leading us further away from true productivity and fulfillment? In this chapter, we will delve deep into the truth behind 24/7 productivity and explore whether it is a sustainable and effective approach in the long run.

The Myth of Productivity:

Before we dissect the myth of 24/7 productivity, we must first understand what true productivity entails. Productivity is not about the sheer number of hours we spend working or the constant state of busyness we find ourselves in. Rather, it is about the efficient and effective use of our time to accomplish meaningful goals and make progress in our personal and professional lives.

Contrary to popular belief, humans are not designed to be machines that can work continuously without breaks or rest. Our brains and bodies need downtime to recharge, reflect, and rejuvenate. However, the allure of constant productivity can make us believe that if we aren't constantly engaged in work, we are somehow falling behind.

The Fallacy of Multitasking:

One of the keys to understanding 24/7 productivity is debunking the fallacy of multitasking. Many people believe that by juggling multiple tasks simultaneously, they can achieve more in less time. However, research has consistently shown that multitasking actually decreases productivity and leads to a higher likelihood of errors and mistakes.

When we try to do multiple things at once, our attention becomes divided, and we fail to give each task the focus and dedication it deserves. Our brains are wired to handle one task at a time efficiently. By attempting to multitask, we not only compromise the quality of our work, but we also drain our mental energy and increase the risk of burnout.

The Importance of Rest and Recovery:

To maintain sustainable productivity, we must recognize the critical role that rest and recovery play in our overall well-being. Rest is not a sign of slacking off; it is an essential component of a healthy and productive life. Studies have shown that regular breaks and adequate sleep improve cognitive function, memory, and problem-solving abilities.

When we neglect rest, we enter a vicious cycle of diminishing returns. Our productivity declines, as does the quality of our work. In contrast, taking periodic breaks from work allows us to recharge our mental batteries, gain clarity, and approach tasks with renewed focus and enthusiasm. By honoring our need for rest, we can achieve more during our productive hours and prevent burnout.

The Danger of Unrealistic Expectations:

The constant pursuit of 24/7 productivity also exposes us to the danger of setting unrealistic expectations for ourselves. Society's glorification of constant busyness can make us feel guilty for taking time off or enjoying leisure activities. This mindset leads to a perpetual state of stress and anxiety, fueled by the fear of not measuring up to societal standards.

It is crucial to redefine our notion of productivity and establish realistic expectations for ourselves. Simply being busy does not equate to being productive. Instead, we should focus on setting meaningful goals, prioritizing tasks, and embracing a healthy work-life balance. By aligning our actions with our values and not succumbing to societal pressures, we can find fulfillment and true productivity within a sustainable framework.

The Power of Deep Work:

One of the most effective antidotes to the 24/7 productivity mindset is the concept of deep work. Coined by author and professor Cal Newport, deep work refers to the ability to focus without distraction on cognitively demanding tasks. It is about delving into a state of flow, where time seems to fly by, and remarkable progress is made.

Deep work requires periods of uninterrupted, concentrated focus. By eliminating and minimizing distractions, such as social media, email notifications, and constant multitasking, we create a conducive environment for deep work to thrive. Instead of striving for constant productivity, it is more valuable to allocate dedicated periods of time to engage in deep work, as this is where our most impactful work truly happens.

The pursuit of 24/7 productivity is a fallacy that can lead us down a path of exhaustion, burnout, and unfulfillment. True productivity involves efficient time management, rest, and prioritization. By embracing the importance of rest, debunking the myth of multitasking, and adopting the practice of deep work, we can establish a sustainable and effective approach to productivity. Let us break free from the cycle of constant busyness and redefine productivity in a way that supports our well-being, creativity, and long-term success.

Time Quality vs. Time Quantity

Time, the most enigmatic concept that has baffled humanity since the beginning of civilization. It is a profound force that governs our lives, dictating the rhythm of our days and shaping our perceptions of reality. Throughout history, scholars, philosophers, and ordinary individuals have grappled with the question of time, seeking to understand its essence and how we can best utilize it. In this chapter, we will explore the intriguing dichotomy between time quality and time quantity, delving into their significance, implications, and how they affect our well-being and productivity.

Defining Time Quality and Time Quantity:

Before we dive deeper into this fascinating subject matter, it is crucial to define the twin concepts at the heart of our discussion - time quality and time quantity.

Time quantity refers to the sheer amount of time available to us. It is the raw material from which we mold our daily experiences, the hours, minutes, and seconds ticking away on our clocks. It is often measured in concrete terms, such as hours spent at work, time dedicated to hobbies, or hours of sleep obtained in a night.

On the other hand, time quality encompasses the subjective experience of time. It focuses not only on the amount of time spent but also on the depth of our engagement and the intrinsic value derived from our activities. It is the difference between being busy and being productive, between mindlessly passing the hours and immersing oneself in a meaningful endeavor.

The Myth of Time Quantity:

In our modern society, the pursuit of time quantity has become an obsession. We are constantly bombarded with messages urging us to work longer hours, sacrifice leisure time, and constantly strive for more. We have been conditioned to believe that the key to success lies in the sheer volume of work we accomplish, measuring our worth by the number of items checked off our to-do lists.

However, this fixation on time quantity has severe consequences for our well-being. As we chase after an elusive sense of accomplishment, we often neglect to consider the quality of the time we devote to our pursuits, leading to burnout, stress, and a sense of emptiness. It is as if we are racing against an invisible clock, never fully savoring the present moment or finding fulfillment in our endeavors.

The Essence of Time Quality:

Time quality, on the other hand, invites us to delve deeper into the fabric of our existence. When we prioritize time quality, we seek to cultivate experiences that are rooted in authenticity, purpose, and personal growth. This means engaging fully in activities that align with our values, interests, and aspirations.

Indeed, when we quality over quantity, we are more likely to lose ourselves in the flow of our work, finding joy, and a sense of fulfillment in the present moment. Time seems to expand as we become fully absorbed in our endeavors, rendering the limits of the clock irrelevant. It is in these moments that we create our most profound achievements, cultivate deeper relationships, and experience true contentment.

Balancing Quality and Quantity:

While the dichotomy between time quality and time quantity may seem stark, achieving a healthy balance between the two is key to leading a fulfilling life. It is essential to acknowledge that both concepts are intertwined and should not be regarded as mutually exclusive. Balancing quality and quantity requires a careful consideration of our priorities, routines, and overall approach to time management.

One approach to achieving balance is to redefine our relationship with time altogether. Instead of seeing time as a limited resource to be managed, we can shift our perspective to view it as an abundant and expansive force available to us. This mental shift allows us to approach our tasks and activities with a sense of abundance and possibility, ultimately improving the quality of our experiences.

Moreover, we must learn to prioritize our activities based on their inherent value and align them with our long-term goals and aspirations. By concentrating on tasks that have a higher impact, rather than filling our schedules with trivialities, we can optimize our use of time and create more meaningful outcomes. This means saying no to certain commitments and consciously allocating our time to endeavors that truly matter to us.

Cultivating Mindfulness:

An essential tool in the pursuit of balance between time quality and time quantity is the practice of mindfulness. Mindfulness involves being fully present and aware of our thoughts, emotions, and sensations in any given moment without judgment or attachment. By cultivating mindfulness, we can bring a heightened sense of awareness and intentionality to our daily lives, allowing us to make conscious choices about how we spend our time.

When we approach each moment with mindfulness, we unlock the potential for true time quality. We become attuned to our own needs and desires, enabling us to direct our energy towards activities that nourish our souls and foster personal growth. This heightened awareness also helps us recognize the moments when we are mindlessly filling our time with distractions or engaging in activities that no longer serve us, allowing for course correction and intentional decision-making.

The dichotomy between time quality and time quantity is a multidimensional topic that elicits profound contemplation. By examining these concepts through a thoughtful lens, we can begin to reshape our relationship with time and unlock its transformative power. By balancing time quality and quantity, prioritizing meaningful engagement, and cultivating mindfulness, we can embark on a journey of personal growth, fulfillment, and true appreciation for the enigma that is time.

Temporal Boundaries for Work and Life

In the modern digital age, the boundaries between work and personal life have become increasingly blurred. As technology enables us to be constantly connected, the distinction between work hours and personal time has eroded, leading to a host of negative consequences. Maintaining healthy temporal boundaries between work and life is essential for overall well-being and productivity. In this chapter, we will explore the importance of temporal boundaries, the challenges in maintaining them, and strategies to establish a healthy work-life balance.

The Nature of Work in the Digital Era:

Before delving into the complexities of temporal boundaries, it is crucial to understand the profound changes brought about by the digital revolution. Traditional work structures, such as the standard 9-to-5 schedule, have been disrupted by the advent of remote work, flexible hours, and global connectivity. This newfound flexibility has its advantages, offering individuals greater autonomy and the ability to work from any location. However, it has also led to a constant pressure to be available and responsive, blurring the lines between professional responsibilities and personal life.

The Importance of Temporal Boundaries:

Maintaining clear boundaries between work and personal life is essential for both individual well-being and productivity. When these boundaries become fuzzy, the negative impact on mental health, relationships, and job performance can be significant. The human brain requires time for rest, recuperation, and engaging in non-work activities. Without these mental breaks, exhaustion, burnout, and diminished creativity become all too common.

Additionally, blurred temporal boundaries can strain personal relationships. When work encroaches on personal time, individuals often have less availability for quality time with family and friends. This imbalance can lead to feelings of resentment and a weakened support system.

Furthermore, recent research has highlighted the long-term detrimental effects of persistent work intruding into personal life. Chronic stress and fatigue can contribute to physical ailments, such as cardiovascular disease, obesity, and compromised immune system functioning. Hence, establishing and maintaining temporal boundaries is critical for overall well-being.

Challenges in Establishing Temporal Boundaries:

Establishing effective temporal boundaries can be a daunting task in today's fast-paced and interconnected world. Several obstacles can impede our ability to create and maintain a healthy work-life balance:

1. Digital Connectivity: Constant access to work emails, instant messaging, and cellphones makes it challenging to disconnect from professional responsibilities. The fear of missing out or not meeting expectations can lead individuals to check their devices obsessively, encroaching on personal time.

2. Unrealistic Workload: Many professionals face an overwhelming workload, leading them to believe they need to be available round-the-clock. The pressure to excel, meet deadlines, and demonstrate dedication can create an unsustainable cycle that erodes boundaries.

3. Organizational Culture: Company cultures that prioritize constant availability and respond to requests at all hours contribute to a culture where blurred temporal boundaries become the norm. Employees might feel compelled to be "always on" to meet perceived expectations, perpetuating the cycle.

Strategies to Establish and Maintain Boundaries:

Despite the challenges, it is possible to establish and maintain healthy temporal boundaries between work and personal life. Here are some strategies to consider:

1. Define Your "Non-Negotiable" Time: Identify specific hours or days in your schedule that are exclusively for personal activities and stick to them. Communicate these boundaries clearly to your colleagues, supervisors, and clients, establishing the expectation that you will not be available during those times, except for emergencies.

2. Utilize Technology Effectively: While technology can blur boundaries, it can also be used to enforce them. Set up automatic "out of office" replies, enable "do not disturb" modes on your devices during non-work hours, and prioritize notifications to reduce distractions. By consciously managing technology, you regain control over when and how you interact with work-related tasks.

3. Establish Clear Work Agreements: Negotiate expectations regarding your work hours and availability with your supervisor or team members. Define what constitutes an emergency or urgent matter that warrants contact outside of regular work hours. By openly discussing boundaries and clarifying expectations, you are more likely to maintain a healthy work-life balance.

4. Practice Mindfulness: Regularly engage in mindfulness exercises to cultivate self-awareness and presence. By being fully present in the moment, you can resist the temptation to check work-related matters during personal time. Techniques such as meditation and deep breathing can help create a mental separation between work and personal life.

5. Set Physical Boundaries: Create physical spaces dedicated to work and personal activities. Designate a specific area of your home for work-related tasks, ideally separate from the spaces where you relax or spend time with loved ones. These physical boundaries can help signal your brain when it's time to shift gears and switch between work and personal life.

In an era where work has permeated our personal lives, establishing and maintaining temporal boundaries is crucial for our well-being and success. By recognizing the negative consequences of blurred boundaries, identifying the challenges we face, and implementing effective strategies, we can regain control over our time and create a healthier work-life balance. It is within our power to set limits, redefine expectations, and reshape the future of work, where boundaries are respected, and personal lives are nurtured alongside professional ambitions.

Time Management in a Digital Age

In today's fast-paced and technology-driven world, time seems to be perpetually slipping away, leaving many people feeling overwhelmed and stressed. The rise of the digital age has brought with it numerous benefits, but it has also introduced new challenges when it comes to managing our time effectively. With the constant barrage of distractions and demands for our attention, it has become increasingly crucial to develop strategies for navigating this digital era while maintaining our productivity and well-being. In this chapter, we will explore the concept of time management in a digital age, outlining practical tips and insights to help you regain control over your time and establish a healthy balance between technology and productivity.

Understanding the Digital Age

Before delving into the strategies for time management, it is essential to understand the impact of the digital age on our lives. The advancements in technology have undoubtedly transformed the way we live, work, and communicate. With smartphones, social media platforms, and countless other digital tools at our fingertips, we are constantly connected to a world buzzing with information and distractions. While these innovations have provided tremendous convenience and possibilities, they have also contributed to a reality where our attention is constantly pulled in multiple directions.

The Perils of Digital Distractions

One of the greatest challenges in time management within the digital age is the prevalence of distractions. Whether it's notifications from social media apps, email alerts, or the allure of endlessly scrolling through news articles, our attention is continuously at risk of being hijacked. Research has shown that these distractions can have a significant impact on our focus and productivity, as it takes valuable time and mental energy to refocus after each interruption. To effectively manage our time, it becomes necessary to recognize and minimize these distractions.

Creating a Digital Detox Ritual

Implementing a digital detox ritual can be a game-changer when it comes to reclaiming control over your time. Designate specific periods throughout the day when you completely disconnect from your devices. During these breaks, you can engage in activities that promote relaxation and mindfulness, such as taking a walk in nature, reading, or practicing meditation. By intentionally disconnecting from the digital world, you allow yourself the opportunity to recharge and refocus, leading to increased productivity and improved overall well-being.

Mastering the Art of Prioritization

In a digital age characterized by information overload, mastering the art of prioritization is essential. With a seemingly infinite number of tasks and commitments vying for our attention, it becomes crucial to identify what truly matters. Start by setting clear goals and objectives, both short-term and long-term, to provide a framework for decision-making. Next, break down these goals into smaller, manageable tasks, assigning priorities based on urgency and importance. By focusing your time and energy on what aligns with your goals, you can avoid becoming overwhelmed by the constant flood of information and demands.

Leveraging Technology to Enhance Productivity

Although technology can be a source of distraction, it also offers a plethora of tools that can significantly enhance productivity and time management. Take advantage of applications and software designed to streamline your workflow, such as project management tools, calendar apps, and note-taking platforms. These tools can help you stay organized, track your progress, and ensure that you are making the most efficient use of your time. However, it's crucial to strike a balance and not let these tools become additional sources of distraction.

Implementing the Pomodoro Technique

One popular technique for managing time effectively in the digital age is the Pomodoro Technique, developed by Francesco Cirillo. This technique involves breaking your work into focused intervals, typically 25 minutes, called "pomodoros," followed by a short break. By working in short bursts, you can maintain higher levels of focus and productivity while preventing burnout. Additionally, by setting specific tasks for each pomodoro and tracking your progress, you gain a sense of accomplishment and motivation, leading to increased efficiency and time management.

Establishing Boundaries and Practicing Saying "No"

In a digital age where our devices enable constant communication and accessibility, it becomes crucial to establish boundaries and learn to say "no" when necessary. Being available 24/7 can quickly lead to burnout and a lack of personal time. Set clear limitations on when and how you will engage with devices and communications. Communicate these boundaries to colleagues, friends, and family to ensure they understand your limitations and respect your need for uninterrupted focus time. Remember, your time is valuable, and learning to say "no" to non-essential tasks or commitments is essential for maintaining balance and effectiveness.

Finding the Right Balance Between Digital and Analog

While the digital age offers tremendous advantages, it's important not to neglect the benefits of analog tools and experiences. In a world dominated by screens, consider incorporating analog elements into your daily routine. Use a physical planner or notebook alongside your digital tools to enhance organization and creativity. Engage in activities that don't rely on technology, such as reading physical books, taking up a hobby that encourages hands-on involvement, or spending quality time with loved ones without digital distractions. By finding the right balance between digital and analog, you can cultivate a more well-rounded approach to managing time and enjoying life.

Time management in a digital age is an ongoing journey that requires constant adaptation and refinement. By recognizing the impact of technology on our lives, understanding the perils of digital distractions, and implementing practical strategies, we can regain control over our time and establish a healthier relationship with technology. Whether it involves creating a digital detox ritual, mastering prioritization, leveraging technology to enhance productivity, or finding balance between digital and analog, these strategies will help you simplify your life, increase productivity, and reclaim the precious time that often slips away.

Chapter 7: Time Management in Relationships and Networking

In today's fast-paced world, effective time management has become crucial for success and personal fulfillment in various aspects of life. One area where it plays a significant role is in relationships and networking. Whether it's maintaining healthy personal connections or building a strong professional network, mastering the art of time management can help individuals navigate these spheres with grace and efficiency. In this chapter, we will explore various strategies and techniques that can be employed to manage time effectively in relationships and networking, enabling individuals to strike a harmonious balance between these important areas of their lives.

The Importance of Time Management in Relationships:

Time is a limited resource, and how we choose to allocate it can have a profound impact on the quality of our relationships. Whether it is our romantic partner, family members, or close friends, investing time and effort is essential for nurturing and strengthening these bonds. However, competing demands and responsibilities often leave individuals feeling drained and struggling to find time for these relationships. Hence, effective time management becomes vital.

One critical aspect of time management in relationships is setting priorities. Reflect on your values and identify the relationships that matter most to you. By doing so, you can allocate your time accordingly, ensuring that these connections receive the attention they deserve. Additionally, consider implementing strategies such as scheduling regular date nights with your partner or establishing dedicated family time to prevent relationships from inadvertently being neglected.

Another aspect of time management in relationships involves effective communication. By openly discussing your time constraints and commitments with your loved ones, you can create a shared understanding and avoid unnecessary conflicts. Furthermore, being fully present during quality time is equally important. Multitasking or constantly checking your phone can send unintended messages of disinterest or disrespect, hindering the growth of the relationship.

Time Management in Networking:

Networking plays a pivotal role in both personal and professional spheres. It allows individuals to tap into a supportive community, gain new insights, and explore opportunities for growth. However, networking events and activities require significant time investment, and without effective time management, it can become overwhelming and unproductive.

Begin by setting clear goals for your networking efforts. Define what you hope to achieve and identify the areas you want to focus on. By doing so, you can allocate your time and energy to activities that align with your objectives, thus making your networking efforts more targeted and productive.

Prioritizing networking activities is also essential. Determine the events and opportunities that are likely to yield the greatest results based on your goals and interests. This way, you can avoid spreading yourself too thin and focus on engagements that have the highest potential for building meaningful connections.

In addition to setting priorities, effective time management in networking involves maintaining a healthy balance. Networking is not solely about attending events or building a web of contacts. It also encompasses nurturing and sustaining these connections over time. Set aside specific time slots in your schedule for following up with new contacts, connecting with established ones, and engaging in meaningful conversations. Strive for quality over quantity, targeting relationships that have mutual benefits and align with your overall objectives.

Challenges and Strategies for Effective Time Management:

Balancing time between relationships and networking can present its fair share of challenges. Identifying and addressing these obstacles can greatly contribute to managing time efficiently in these areas.

One challenge often encountered is the fear of missing out (FOMO). The fear of missing opportunities or falling behind in one's personal or professional life can lead individuals to overextend themselves, leaving little time for relationships or effective networking. To overcome this challenge, develop a clear understanding of your priorities, values, and goals. By aligning your time allocations with these components, you can confidently say no to opportunities that do not align with your interests or long-term objectives.

Another challenge is the balancing act between personal and professional commitments. Often, time spent at work or on career-related activities can encroach upon personal relationships and networking. Employing strategies such as effective delegation, time blocking, and effective communication with your employer, partner, or team can help strike a better balance.

Quality Time in Personal Relationships

In our modern, fast-paced world, it seems that time is always in short supply. We find ourselves constantly juggling multiple responsibilities, struggling to strike a balance between work, family, and personal commitments. Often, amidst this chaos, our personal relationships suffer, and we forget to invest in the most essential aspect of any successful relationship: quality time. In this chapter, we will explore the significance of quality time in personal relationships, its impact on our emotional well-being, and how to create meaningful and memorable moments with our loved ones.

Understanding Quality Time:

Quality time refers to the period spent engaging in meaningful activities with another person, where the focus is on building a deep emotional connection rather than simply passing the time. It involves being present, attentive, and truly invested in the person and the moment. Quality time allows individuals to strengthen their emotional bond, foster mutual understanding, and create memories that sustain relationships in difficult times.

The Importance of Quality Time:

1. Nurtures Emotional Connection:
Spending quality time with our loved ones provides a unique opportunity to nurture the emotional connection we share. It allows us to express our love, support, and appreciation for one another. By being present and engaged in these moments, we validate the importance of our relationship and reinforce the trust that underlies it.

2. Enhances Communication and Understanding:
Meaningful conversations and shared activities during quality time enable effective communication and understanding between individuals. When we dedicate uninterrupted time to our loved ones, we create a safe space for open and honest dialogue. Through such conversations, we can express ourselves, clarify misunderstandings, and gain insight into each other's perspectives.

3. Creates Lasting Memories:
Quality time offers a chance to create lasting memories that become the foundation of our relationship. By sharing experiences, engaging in shared hobbies, or embarking on adventures together, we forge connections that can be cherished and recalled during challenging times. These memories serve as a reminder of the love and joy we experience with our loved ones.

4. Fosters a Sense of Belonging and Security:

When we spend quality time with someone, we send them a powerful message - that they are important, cherished, and valued. This, in turn, fosters a sense of belonging and security. Knowing that we have someone truly invested in our well-being helps us navigate the ups and downs of life with greater resilience and strength.

Creating Quality Time:

Now that we understand the significance of quality time, let's explore some practical ways to create moments that genuinely enhance our personal relationships.

1. Prioritize and Schedule:

In our busy lives, it is crucial to prioritize quality time and set aside specific periods for it. By scheduling activities, dates, or dedicated bonding time in advance, we ensure that it becomes an integral part of our routine. By treating quality time as a non-negotiable commitment, we make it a priority and demonstrate its value to our loved ones.

2. Be Present and Mindful:

During quality time, it is vital to be fully present and engaged. Put away distractions such as smartphones, turn off the television, or step away from work-related concerns. Show genuine interest, actively listen, and be mindful of non-verbal cues. This level of presence and attentiveness communicates our desire to connect deeply with the other person.

3. Shared Interests and Activities:

Engaging in shared interests and activities is a powerful way to bond during quality time. It can be as simple as cooking together, going for a hike, or taking up a new hobby that both individuals are excited about. Engaging in activities that bring joy to both parties allows for a deeper connection and creates a positive environment for strengthening the relationship.

4. Intentional Communication:

Open and intentional communication is key to quality time. In these moments, it is important to actively listen, express oneself honestly, and practice empathy. Ask open-ended questions, share your feelings, and demonstrate support and understanding. These intentional conversations build trust and help deepen the emotional connection between individuals.

5. Be Spontaneous:

While scheduling quality time is essential, allowing for spontaneity and surprise adds excitement and novelty to the relationship. Surprise your loved one with a spontaneous picnic in the park or plan a surprise adventure. The element of surprise enhances anticipation and adds an extra layer of joy to the experience.

Efficient Networking Techniques

Networking is a crucial aspect of our modern world. In both personal and professional spheres, the ability to build and maintain a network of connections is vital for success. However, with the ever-increasing digital landscape and the constant influx of information, it can be challenging to navigate effectively and efficiently. In this chapter, we will explore various techniques and strategies that can help you optimize your networking endeavors, ensuring maximum efficiency in both time and effort.

1. Define Your Networking Goals

Before embarking on any networking journey, it is important to clearly define your objectives. Are you looking to expand your professional network, find new job opportunities, or gather information for a specific project? Understanding your goals will help you narrow down your focus and streamline your networking efforts. By having a clear direction, you can prioritize your time and energy on connections that align with your objectives.

2. Utilize Online Platforms

The digital age has revolutionized networking possibilities, offering numerous online platforms to connect with individuals across the globe. Leveraging social media platforms such as LinkedIn, Twitter, and Facebook can be incredibly effective in expanding your network. These platforms enable you to highlight your skills and experience, engage in industry-related discussions, and connect with professionals in your field.

When using online platforms, be mindful of the content you share and the way you interact with others. Present yourself in a genuine and professional manner, making sure your online presence aligns with your networking goals. Regularly engage with your connections by commenting on their posts, sharing valuable content, and participating in groups and discussions. By actively participating and contributing to the online community, you can establish yourself as a credible and reliable source of information.

3. Attend Networking Events

While online networking is convenient and effective, nothing can replace the value of face-to-face interactions. Attending industry-specific conferences, trade shows, and meetups allows you to connect with like-minded individuals who share your interests. These events provide an excellent opportunity to establish meaningful connections, exchange business cards, and engage in in-depth conversations.

To make the most out of networking events, come prepared. Familiarize yourself with the event schedule, keynote speakers, and attending organizations. Research the backgrounds of key individuals you would like to connect with, enabling you to initiate relevant conversations. Dress professionally, carry a stack of well-designed business cards, and be ready to actively listen and engage with other attendees. Remember, networking events are not solely about self-promotion. Offer assistance, provide value, and make genuine connections that extend beyond superficial introductions.

4. Leverage Existing Relationships

Networking is not only about creating new connections but also nurturing and leveraging existing relationships. Your current network can be a powerful resource for introductions and referrals. Reaching out to individuals you already have a connection with can be less daunting and more productive than cold networking.

Consider organizing networking lunches or coffee meetings with individuals from your existing network. Express your interest in learning about their current projects, challenges, and goals. By actively listening and offering assistance, you can strengthen your existing relationship while potentially expanding your network through their connections. Remember to reciprocate by offering your knowledge, experiences, or contacts whenever possible.

5. Seek Diversity in Your Network

It is easy to fall into the trap of connecting with individuals who are similar to us in terms of background, interests, or profession. While it's essential to maintain connections within your immediate community, seeking diversity in your network can bring fresh perspectives and opportunities.

Look for connections outside of your usual circles. Seek out individuals with different backgrounds, industries, or areas of expertise. Engaging with diverse people can provide unique insights and opportunities for collaboration, leading to innovative solutions or unexpected opportunities. Remember, networking is about expanding your horizons and uncovering new possibilities.

6. Nurture Your Network

Building a network is not a one-time event but an ongoing process that requires nurturing and maintenance. Make it a habit to regularly reach out to your connections, even if it's a simple check-in or sharing an article you think they might find interesting. Take the time to attend birthdays, anniversaries, and milestones of your contacts. Celebrating their achievements and showing genuine interest in their lives will solidify your connections.

Additionally, consider organizing gatherings or events aimed at bringing your network together. By creating a platform for professionals in your network to interact and collaborate, you can strengthen bonds and foster a community that supports each other's goals.

7. Follow Up and Follow Through

A critical aspect of efficient networking is following up and following through. After meeting someone new, send a personalized follow-up email or message expressing your gratitude for the conversation. Reference specific topics or points from your discussion to demonstrate your attentiveness and engagement. Following through on promises or commitments made during your conversation showcases your reliability and professionalism.

Remember, networking is a two-way street. Don't hesitate to reach out and offer your assistance or insight to your connections when you can add value. By actively engaging and supporting your network, you cultivate a circle of individuals who are more likely to reciprocate and offer their help when you need it.

Efficient networking is an art that requires strategic planning, genuine engagement, and a commitment to building lasting connections. By defining your networking goals, utilizing online platforms, attending networking events, leveraging existing relationships, seeking diversity, nurturing your network, and following up diligently, you can optimize your networking efforts and unlock countless opportunities.

Temporal Investments in Lasting Bonds

In the realm of personal relationships, we often tend to focus on the present moment, seeking immediate gratification and quick fixes. But, what if we shift our perspective and consider the value of making temporal investments for lasting bonds? At the core of any healthy and enduring relationship lies the willingness to invest time, effort, and energy. In this chapter, we will delve into the concept of temporal investments and explore how they contribute to fostering deeper connections and building lasting bonds.

Understanding Temporal Investments

Temporal investments can be best understood as the intentional allocation of one's time and energy into nurturing relationships. Just as we invest our financial resources to secure our future, temporal investments are akin to emotional investments that yield long-term rewards. But what sets them apart from mere fleeting gestures is their ability to transcend the superficial and create an enduring bond rooted in trust, reciprocity, and love.

The Importance of Consistency

When it comes to temporal investments, consistency is key. Lasting bonds require a regular and sustained effort to thrive. Much like tending to a garden, if we neglect our relationships and only sporadically invest in them, they will wither and gradually fade away. A healthy relationship necessitates consistent communication, quality time, and empathetic understanding. By showing up consistently, we signal to our loved ones that they are a priority in our lives, fostering a sense of security and stability.

Quality Time: Beyond the Clock

While investing time in relationships is vital, it is equally important to emphasize the quality of that time rather than solely focusing on quantity. In our fast-paced world, it seems that we are always squeezed for time, leading to a misguided belief that spending hours together equates to nurturing connections. However, quality time goes beyond mere physical presence. It involves being fully engaged, actively listening to one another, and genuinely sharing experiences. Investing quality time allows us to create cherished memories and fosters a deeper sense of emotional intimacy.

The Power of Active Listening

Actively listening to our loved ones is an often overlooked yet crucial skill in temporal investments. Too often, we find ourselves lost in our own thoughts or distracted by the countless notifications of the digital realm. However, active listening requires us to be present, to truly pay attention to the words being spoken, and to convey our genuine interest through nonverbal cues. By empathetically listening to our loved ones, we demonstrate that their thoughts, feelings, and experiences matter to us, deepening the bonds we share.

Support and Empathy: The Building Blocks of Trust

Investing time in our relationships means being there for one another in times of both joy and sorrow. Building strong bonds involves providing unwavering support and empathy, acting as a stable foundation for trust to grow. By showing up during challenging moments, we not only help our loved ones weather the storm but also demonstrate our commitment to their well-being. Investing time in cultivating empathy allows us to better understand their needs, fears, and desires, fostering an environment where openness and vulnerability can flourish.

Shared Experiences: Creating a Tapestry of Memories

As social beings, we crave shared experiences that contribute to the mosaic of our lives. Temporal investments enable us to create a rich tapestry of memories together, strengthening the bonds between us. Whether it's embarking on adventures, celebrating milestones, or simply engaging in everyday activities, shared experiences create a sense of belonging and togetherness. Such shared moments become the threads that intertwine our stories, forging lasting bonds that can weather the test of time.

The Art of Selflessness

Investing time and energy into our relationships requires an element of selflessness. It entails prioritizing the needs and desires of our loved ones alongside our own. True temporal investments involve acts of kindness, thoughtfulness, and sacrifice. Yet, it is important to maintain a healthy balance, ensuring that our own well-being is not compromised. Striking this delicate equilibrium allows us to invest in others while also nurturing our own growth and happiness.

As we conclude this chapter on temporal investments in lasting bonds, it is crucial to recognize the transformative power they have to enrich our relationships. By consistently investing quality time, actively listening, providing support and empathy, sharing experiences, and practicing selflessness, we cultivate deeper connections that stand the test of time. Temporal investments are an ongoing journey, requiring patience, commitment, and a genuine desire to nourish the bonds that enrich our lives. So, let us embark on this journey and discover the beauty of investing in relationships that will leave an indelible mark on our hearts.

Time-Saving Communication Hacks

In today's fast-paced world, effective communication plays a crucial role in our personal and professional lives. Whether we are connecting with colleagues, friends, or family, the ability to convey messages clearly and efficiently is essential. However, with the constant distractions and information overload that surround us, finding time for meaningful conversations can be a daunting task. In this chapter, we will explore a collection of time-saving communication hacks that will help you streamline your daily interactions, improve your productivity, and allow you to make the most of your precious time.

1. Prioritize Your Communication Channels

With the vast array of communication tools available to us, it's easy to get overwhelmed. Email, messaging apps, social media, and phone calls bombard us with notifications and demands for attention. To optimize your time, it is crucial to prioritize and master the channels that work best for you.

Start by identifying the channels that are most commonly used by your important contacts, whether it be email, Slack, or phone calls. Focus on those preferred channels and set clear boundaries on when and how you engage with them. By cutting out unnecessary noise and streamlining your communication channels, you can save valuable time and avoid getting lost in a sea of messages.

2. Utilize Email Filters and Templates

Email is a powerful tool, but if not managed efficiently, it can quickly become a time sink. To tame your overflowing inbox, make use of filters and templates.

Set up filters to automatically sort incoming emails into folders based on criteria such as sender, subject, or keywords. This way, you can prioritize and address important messages while leaving less critical ones for later review. Additionally, create email templates for common responses or inquiries. A well-curated collection of templates will save you from typing repetitive messages, allowing you to quickly reply to emails in a fraction of the time.

3. Leverage Voice-to-Text Technology

Typing can be time-consuming, especially when faced with lengthy messages or documents. Instead of typing everything out, consider using voice-to-text technology. Most smartphones and computers have built-in voice recognition software that can transcribe your spoken words into text accurately.

Whether you're drafting an email, writing a report, or even composing a text message, speaking your thoughts aloud can significantly speed up the process. Additionally, this method can be particularly useful when multitasking, allowing you to dictate your ideas while accomplishing other tasks simultaneously.

4. Master the Art of Quick and Effective Meetings

Meetings are notorious for consuming excessive amounts of time, often leaving us with less time for actual work. By implementing a few strategies, you can transform your meetings into efficient and productive sessions.

Start by setting clear agendas and objectives for each meeting, indicating precisely what needs to be accomplished. Share these agendas in advance, giving participants time to prepare and allowing them to determine whether their presence is essential. During the meeting, stick to the agenda, keeping discussions focused and time-limited.

Consider implementing "stand-up" meetings whenever possible. These meetings, often kept short and concise, involve participants staying on their feet rather than sitting down. By eliminating the comfort of chairs, participants are more likely to keep discussions brief and prevent unnecessary tangents.

5. Embrace the Power of Synchronous and Asynchronous Communication

Not all conversations require immediate responses. By embracing both synchronous and asynchronous communication, you can strike a balance between responsiveness and efficiency.

Synchronous communication, such as phone calls or face-to-face meetings, allows for real-time interaction and immediate decision-making. However, it often requires simultaneous availability, which can be challenging to coordinate, especially with remote or international team members.

Asynchronous communication, on the other hand, allows participants to engage when it's most convenient for them. Email, messaging apps, and project management tools all provide channels for asynchronous communication. By utilizing these tools, you can reduce interruptions, provide thoughtful responses, and avoid the constant need to be "always-on."

6. Apply the 5-Sentence Rule

When engaging in written communication, whether it's an email, a report, or a presentation, the temptation to overcomplicate and over-explain can be strong. To save time and keep your messages concise, consider applying the 5-sentence rule.

Challenge yourself to convey your message effectively within five sentences. This forces you to be clear, succinct, and ensure your key points are communicated efficiently. By adopting this approach, you not only save time for yourself but also for your recipients, who will appreciate brief and to-the-point messages.

7. Employ Visual Communication Tools

Sometimes, a picture is worth a thousand words. Visual communication tools can help you convey complex ideas or emotions succinctly, saving time and eliminating potential misunderstandings. Consider utilizing tools like infographics, flowcharts, or mind-mapping software to present information in a visually appealing and easily comprehensible way. These visual aids can make your messages more engaging and memorable, leading to more effective communication overall.

Mastering the art of time-saving communication is a skill that can greatly enhance both your personal and professional life. By prioritizing your communication channels, utilizing filters and templates, leveraging voice-to-text technology, and applying other time-saving hacks, you can create more streamlined and efficient interactions. Remember that effective communication should not be compromised in the pursuit of saving time. Instead, each tip presented in this chapter aims to enhance your communication practices and help you find the perfect balance between effectiveness and productivity.

Chapter 8: Long-Term Planning and Temporal Vision

In the fast-paced world we live in, it's easy to get caught up in the day-to-day tasks and lose sight of the bigger picture. This is where long-term planning and temporal vision come into play. In this chapter, we will explore the importance of long-term planning, and how developing a temporal vision can help us navigate through the complexities of life.

Understanding Long-Term Planning

Long-term planning refers to the process of setting goals and creating a roadmap to achieve them over an extended period. It involves envisioning the future and making decisions today that will positively impact our tomorrow. By developing a long-term plan, we can align our actions with our aspirations and maximize our chances of success.

Why is Long-Term Planning Important?

Long-term planning is instrumental for personal and professional growth. Without a clear direction or set goals, we can find ourselves aimlessly drifting through life, never truly reaching our full potential. Here are a few reasons why long-term planning is crucial:

1. Clarity and Focus: Long-term planning provides us with clarity about our aspirations and goals. It helps us understand what we truly want in life and enables us to stay focused on our objectives, even when faced with obstacles or distractions.

2. Strategic Decision-Making: When we have a long-term plan, we can make more strategic decisions. By considering the potential long-term consequences of our actions, we avoid impulsive choices that may hinder our progress or lead us astray.

3. Resource Optimization: Long-term planning allows proper allocation of resources. Whether it's time, money, or energy, knowing what we are working towards helps us prioritize and efficiently utilize our resources, leading to increased productivity and overall effectiveness.

Developing a Temporal Vision

A temporal vision is the ability to envision the future in a way that integrates our personal goals and desires with the changing dynamics of the world. It involves understanding the passage of time, anticipating trends, and adapting our plans accordingly. A strong temporal vision enables us to stay ahead of the curve and seize opportunities as they arise.

Components of a Temporal Vision

1. Future Orientation: A temporal vision requires us to focus on the future rather than solely react to the present or dwell on the past. While it's important to learn from our past experiences, consistently looking ahead allows us to shape our desired outcomes.

2. Environmental Awareness: To develop a strong temporal vision, we need to be aware of our surroundings and the factors that influence our lives. This includes staying informed about technological advancements, societal shifts, economic trends, and any other external factors that could impact our long-term plans.

3. Adaptability: A good temporal vision is adaptable. It allows us to adjust our plans as circumstances change and new opportunities emerge. Being rigid and resistant to change can hinder our growth and limit our chances of success.

4. Collaboration: Temporal vision isn't just about personal goals; it involves understanding and aligning with the visions of others. Collaborating with like-minded individuals or groups expands our horizons and increases our chances of achieving collective success.

Applying Long-Term Planning and Temporal Vision

1. Goal Setting: The first step in long-term planning is setting specific, measurable, achievable, relevant, and time-bound (SMART) goals. These goals provide us with a roadmap to follow and act as milestones along our journey.

2. Create Action Plans: Once we have defined our goals, it's essential to break them down into actionable steps. By clearly outlining the strategies and tasks required to achieve each goal, we can maintain focus and track progress.

3. Regular Review and Adjustments: Long-term plans are not set in stone; they require regular review and adjustments. As we progress, circumstances may change, and we may need to realign or modify our plans accordingly. By assessing our progress regularly, we can identify areas that need adjustment and make any necessary changes to stay on track.

4. Embrace Learning Opportunities: Long-term planning and temporal vision require continuous learning. Staying open to new knowledge, seeking feedback, and investing in personal development enhances our understanding of the world and provides us with the tools needed to adapt and thrive.

Monthly and Yearly Temporal Reviews

In our fast-paced lives, it often feels like time is slipping through our fingers. Days turn into weeks, weeks into months, and before we know it, another year has passed. We find ourselves wondering where the time went and whether we made the most of it. This chapter explores the importance of incorporating monthly and yearly temporal reviews into our lives to regain control over our time, reflect on our accomplishments, and set new goals.

Understanding Temporal Reviews

Temporal reviews refer to the practice of regularly evaluating and reflecting upon the passing of time. It involves taking a step back from our daily routines and commitments to gain a broader perspective on our lives. By examining the months and years that have gone by, we can identify patterns, strengths, weaknesses, and opportunities for growth.

Monthly Temporal Reviews

Monthly temporal reviews, as the name suggests, entail reflecting on the events and experiences of the past month. This regular practice empowers us to make intentional adjustments to our daily lives and establish positive habits.

1. Setting the Stage

To conduct a monthly temporal review, set aside a dedicated time and space that encourages focus and solitude. Find a cozy corner with a notebook, a cup of tea, and perhaps some background music that inspires reflection.

2. Recalling the Month's Highlights

Begin by jotting down key highlights and events from the past month. Consider accomplishments, challenges overcome, relationships strengthened, and any transformative experiences. By acknowledging these moments, we gain a sense of gratitude and satisfaction while also identifying areas for improvement.

3. Analyzing Patterns and Trends

Next, analyze any recurring patterns or trends that emerged during the month. Did you notice certain behaviors or activities that either contributed positively or hindered your progress? By understanding these patterns, you can make conscious choices to foster positive habits and shift away from negative ones.

4. Identifying Lessons Learned

Reflect on the lessons you learned during the month. What insights emerged? Did you acquire new skills, knowledge, or perspectives? By extracting powerful lessons, you can apply them in the future to enhance personal growth and development.

5. Celebrating Achievements

Acknowledge your achievements, regardless of their size or significance. Celebrating small wins helps cultivate a mindset of accomplishment and fulfillment, reinforcing positive behaviors and attitudes.

6. Setting New Goals

Based on your reflections, identify one or two actionable and realistic goals for the following month. Visualize what you hope to achieve and determine the steps necessary to get there. By setting clear objectives, you'll maintain momentum and motivation.

Yearly Temporal Reviews

While monthly temporal reviews focus on short-term plans and reflections, yearly temporal reviews shift the lens to encompass the bigger picture. They grant us an opportunity to assess our personal growth, reassess priorities, and refine our life trajectory.

1. Carving Out Dedicated Time

Carve out uninterrupted time for your yearly temporal review. Consider taking a weekend getaway or immersing yourself in a tranquil environment that invites introspection. It's crucial to create an atmosphere that fosters deep thinking and self-analysis.

2. Reflecting on the Year

Begin by reflecting on the past year's accomplishments, challenges, and experiences. How did these events shape you? What were the high and low points? Take note of the emotions that accompany each memory and let those insights guide you.

3. Evaluating Goals and Objectives

Review the goals you set at the beginning of the year. Assess the progress you made and identify any unfulfilled objectives. This evaluation helps determine which goals to carry forward, revise, or discard altogether. It's essential to be adaptable and accept that circumstances may have changed throughout the year.

4. Recognizing Areas for Improvement

Be honest with yourself and identify areas in your life that need improvement. Whether they relate to relationships, health, personal development, or career, acknowledging these shortcomings is the first step toward positive change.

5. Considering New Goals

Once you've evaluated the past year and recognized areas for improvement, set meaningful goals for the upcoming year. These goals should align with your passions, values, and aspirations. Remember to break them down into actionable steps to increase your chances of success.

6. Crafting a Roadmap

Create a roadmap for the year ahead, outlining key milestones and a general plan to achieve your goals. However, remain flexible as unforeseen opportunities and challenges may arise. It's crucial to strike a balance between structure and adaptability.

Incorporating monthly and yearly temporal reviews into our lives provides an invaluable opportunity for growth, self-reflection, and personal development. By taking the time to evaluate our progress, celebrate successes, and set new goals, we can create a more intentional and meaningful life. Embrace the journey of temporal reviews, and watch yourself flourish.

Setting Milestones and Celebrating Time

Time is a fascinating concept that both unifies and separates us. It is a constant force, ticking away with each passing second, yet it can also be subjective, appearing to speed up or slow down depending on our experiences. In the whirlwind of our busy lives, it is crucial to recognize the importance of setting milestones and celebrating time. This chapter explores the significance of milestones in personal and professional development, how to effectively set them, and the various ways we can celebrate and appreciate the passing of time.

Why Set Milestones?

Milestones serve as guideposts on the journey of life. They help us measure our progress, assess our achievements, and provide a sense of direction. By setting milestones, we break down our long-term goals into manageable, actionable steps. Whether it's completing a degree, launching a business, or embarking on a fitness journey, milestones enable us to track our progress and maintain motivation. Without milestones, we risk getting lost in the vast sea of opportunities, losing sight of our objectives, and ultimately diminishing our chances of success.

Choosing the Right Milestones:

Setting milestones is an art that requires careful consideration. The process begins with identifying our long-term goals. Start by visualizing where you want to be in a year, five years, or even a decade. Once the overarching objectives are established, break them down into smaller, realistic milestones. Remember, milestones should be challenging yet attainable to avoid frustration or complacency. Each milestone should be measurable, allowing you to track your progress quantitatively. For example, if your goal is to improve your physical fitness, a measurable milestone could be running a certain distance within a specific time frame. By clearly defining your milestones, you can better understand the steps necessary to achieve them and stay motivated throughout the journey.

Tracking Your Progress:

To effectively utilize milestones, it is essential to track your progress continuously. Record your achievements, no matter how small, as this provides a visual representation of how far you've come. Keep a journal or use technology to monitor your progress, documenting milestones reached, challenges faced, and lessons learned along the way. Regularly reviewing your progress not only provides a sense of accomplishment but also allows for adjustments and modifications if required. Do not be discouraged by temporary setbacks or deviations from the plan. Celebrate the small victories, learn from the obstacles encountered, and keep moving forward.

Celebrating the Passage of Time:

As we set milestones and strive towards our goals, it is equally important to celebrate and appreciate the passage of time. Recognizing our achievements no matter how big or small, helps to foster a positive mindset and creates momentum for further progress. Celebrations need not always be grand or extravagant; sometimes, the simplest gestures can be the most meaningful. Here are a few ideas to celebrate the passing of time:

1. Personal Reflection: Take a moment to reflect on your personal growth and accomplishments. Write a letter to yourself highlighting your achievements and expressing gratitude for the journey. This practice not only provides a sense of closure for completed milestones but also serves as a reminder of the progress made.

2. Gather Loved Ones: Celebrate your milestones with the people who matter most. Organize a small get-together or a family dinner to share your achievements and express gratitude for their support along the way. Surrounding yourself with loved ones not only amplifies the joy of celebration but also strengthens the bonds that uplift and inspire you.

3. Treat Yourself: Reward yourself for reaching your milestones. Treat yourself to a relaxing spa day, indulge in your favorite book or movie, or embark on a short trip to a place you've always wanted to visit. These rewards act as motivators, fueling your determination to

reach the next milestone.

4. Give Back: Celebrating time is not only about personal achievements but also about giving back to others. Take a moment to help those less fortunate by volunteering your time or donating to a charitable cause. Celebrating milestones by making a positive impact on others can be a profoundly rewarding experience.

5. Learn and Grow: Milestones are not just about reaching a destination; they are about the journey itself. Embrace the lessons learned and the skills developed along the way. Continuously educate yourself, attend workshops or seminars, and acquire new skills. By investing in personal development, you are equipping yourself for future milestones and celebrating time by enhancing your own potential.

Setting milestones and celebrating time have profound implications in our personal and professional development. They provide structure, direction, and motivation, fueling our desire to achieve our goals. Milestones break down long-term objectives into actionable steps and give us a sense of progress and accomplishment. Meanwhile, celebrating the passage of time allows us to reflect, express gratitude, and recharge for the next milestone. So, as you continue on your journey, remember to set meaningful milestones, track your progress, and celebrate each passing moment. Life is a collection of moments, and it is up to us to make each one count.

Vision Boards and Temporal Mapping

In our perpetual journey of self-discovery and personal growth, it is essential to have a vision, a blueprint that guides us towards our greatest potential. While our minds can conceive magnificent dreams, our imagination often requires a tangible toolkit to bring them to life. Vision boards and temporal mapping present two powerful techniques that have gained immense popularity for their ability to manifest desires and clarify life goals. In this chapter, we will explore the origins, methodologies, and benefits of these transformative practices and learn how they can propel us towards a purposeful and fulfilled life.

Section 1: Unleashing the Power of Vision Boards

1.1 Origins and Evolution

Vision boards have a rich history spanning centuries, with their roots tracing back to ancient civilizations. The ancient Egyptians, for instance, believed that by visualizing their desires through hieroglyphs and artwork, they could encourage the universe's energies to align with their aspirations. Similarly, Native American tribes used pictorial representations to evoke manifestation and spiritual connection.

In contemporary times, the concept of vision boards gained mainstream attention through the Law of Attraction, popularized by Rhonda Byrne's revolutionary book, "The Secret." The Law of Attraction suggests that what we focus on, we attract into our lives. Vision boards serve as a tangible representation of our desires, keeping our attention and intention fixed on our goals.

1.2 Methodology and Creation Process

Creating a vision board is a deeply personal and creative endeavor. The process involves curating a collage of images, words, and symbols that resonate with our aspirations and desired outcomes. Here are the steps to create an impactful vision board:

a) Clarify Your Intentions: Begin by introspecting and identifying the core desires and goals you want to manifest in your life. These could encompass various aspects, such as career, relationships, health, and personal growth.

b) Gather Inspirational Materials: Collect magazines, photographs, quotes, or even printouts from the internet that visually represent your intentions. Look for images or words that evoke an emotional response, resonating with the essence of your desires.

c) Assemble and Arrange: Let your creativity flow as you arrange these elements on a poster board, a corkboard, or even a digital platform. Arrange and rearrange them until the final composition feels harmonious and visually stimulating.

d) Display and Reflect: Place your completed vision board in a prominent location where you can view it daily. Take time each day to reflect upon the images and symbols, connecting with their energy to keep your focus aligned with your goals.

1.3 The Science and Psychology Behind Vision Boards

Beyond their expressive and artistic appeal, vision boards are rooted in science and psychology. Our brain is naturally wired to respond to visual stimuli, specifically images that invoke emotions and activate the reticular activating system (RAS) – a part of our brain responsible for filtering information.

By exposing ourselves to visual representations of our desires on a daily basis, we signal to our brain that these goals are important to us. Consequently, our RAS filters out irrelevant information and helps us notice opportunities, people, and resources that align with our aspirations. Vision boards create a state of heightened awareness, enabling us to seize these serendipitous moments and manifest our dreams.

Section 2: Temporal Mapping - Charting Your Path to Success

2.1 Understanding Temporal Mapping

Temporal mapping is a complementary technique to vision boards, focusing on the strategic planning and organization of our goals over time. Rather than solely relying on visualization, temporal mapping empowers us to break down our dreams into actionable, time-bound steps.

2.2 Methodology and Execution

a) Define Your Desired Outcomes: Just like with vision boards, clearly articulate the specific goals you wish to achieve, but this time, ensure they are SMART goals – Specific, Measurable, Achievable, Relevant, and Time-bound.

b) Create a Timeline: Break down your goals into smaller milestones with specific deadlines. Consider the short-term, mid-term, and long-term objectives that will lead you closer to your ultimate dream.

c) Identify Necessary Actions: For each milestone, determine the actions required to achieve them. Think about the skills, knowledge, and resources you need to acquire to make progress. Make your action steps as detailed and actionable as possible.

d) Review and Revise: Regularly review your temporal map and adapt it as needed. Life circumstances and priorities evolve, and refining your plan helps you stay aligned with your aspirations.

2.3 The Synergy of Vision Boards and Temporal Mapping

Combining vision boards with temporal mapping creates a powerful synergy that enhances our ability to manifest our dreams. While vision boards ignite our imagination and emotions, temporal mapping provides the structure and strategic guidance needed to transform dreams into reality.

By integrating these techniques, we achieve a holistic and intentional approach to goal achievement. Vision boards keep our minds aligned with our desires, while temporal mapping ensures that we take consistent action steps towards them, optimizing our chances of success.

Section 3: Benefits and Personal Testimonials

3.1 Manifestation and Goal Achievement

Both vision boards and temporal mapping are proven methodologies for manifesting desires and achieving goals. Numerous success stories can be found across the spectrum of personal growth, including improved health, career advancements, thriving relationships, and financial abundance. Acting as a constant reminder of our aspirations, vision boards and temporal mapping serve as beacons guiding us towards our desired outcomes.

3.2 Clarity, Focus, and Motivation

By immersing ourselves in the creation and reflection process of vision boards and temporal mapping, we gain a deep sense of clarity about our path and purpose. These practices help us uncover hidden desires, consolidate our intentions, and maintain focus on what truly matters to us. Moreover, vision boards and temporal mapping fuel motivation as we witness the incremental progress towards our goals, strengthening our resolve to persevere.

Vision boards and temporal mapping offer dynamic and complementary approaches to manifesting our dreams and achieving our goals. Through creative expression and strategic planning, we tap into the power of visualization, self-reflection, and actionable steps. By integrating these transformative techniques into our lives, we unlock our highest potential, aligning our mind, heart, and actions towards a purposeful and fulfilled future.